A Good Soil Life

A Good Soil Life

*Cultivating a Resilient and Whole Heart
in a Hurried World*

MICHELLE AKRAMI

RESOURCE *Publications* · Eugene, Oregon

A GOOD SOIL LIFE
Cultivating a Resilient and Whole Heart in a Hurried World

Resource Publications
An Imprint of Wipf and Stock Publishers
199 W. 8th Ave., Suite 3
Eugene, OR 97401

www.wipfandstock.com

PAPERBACK ISBN: 979-8-3852-4082-1
HARDCOVER ISBN: 979-8-3852-4083-8
EBOOK ISBN: 979-8-3852-4084-5

03/13/25

*To my husband, Cameron,
and our children, Katelyn, Evan, Abigail, Zoey, and Caleb.
May our roots go down deep in the soil of God's marvelous love.
Let's cultivate good soil hearts together all of our lives
for the glory of God.*

Contents

Acknowledgments

THANK YOU TO MY amazing husband, Cameron, and our children, Katelyn, Evan, Abigail, Zoey and Caleb, for cheering me on. To my parents, Jeff and Jennifer Sticka, for their encouragement and prayers. To my mother-in-law, Kathy Akrami, and my beloved late father-in-law, Akbar Akrami. To my brother, Ryan Sticka, and my sister-in-law, Stephanie Sticka. To my brother-in-law, Kevan Akrami, and my sister-in-law, Betania Noguiera.

To Cameron Akrami, Vilppu Anttila, Ashley Lafrenz, and Shelby Quintero for your editing, feedback, and encouragement. To Steven Manuel and Vilppu Anttila for reading my book, checking my theology and encouraging me in this endeavor.

1

Clearing the Beds
(How It All Started)

I LEARNED GARDENING THE hard way as a "green" gardener in my mid-thirties. I tend to be the type of personality that has a free spirit blended with a spontaneous, I'll-figure-it-out-as-I-go-and-even-improvise-with-what-I-have flair. This sometimes leads to . . . interesting outcomes.

During our afternoon family quiet time after church on a Sunday in 2018, I was perusing a new magazine featuring farmhouses, gardening tips, and antiquing. I read an article on growing your own food and decided I wanted to do the same. Right. Now.

Behind the macrame swing I was sitting in was a small array of raised garden beds we had constructed seven years earlier, forgotten and overgrown with weeds up to two feet tall. I abandoned my new magazine and sweet tea and immediately started ripping the weeds out and delivered them to our eager chickens. I was a mama on a mission. I was determined to plant some seeds and grow our own food. The soil in these garden beds was about seven years old. I didn't know anything about soil. I just figured that if you planted a seed in dirt, something was bound to grow . . . right?

Fast-forward four months and I had arugula growing (anemic and spicy for some reason), peas, awkward hollyhocks (placed in the weirdest spot of the garden . . . poor impromptu planning on my part), cilantro, kale, beets, and rosemary. Quite the eclectic collection, yes? I tried to stick to what we would eat (OK, the beets are only for me and *one* of our five children who happens to like them).

Our first garden.

I noticed something perplexing about the beets, though: the top leaves barely grew to about two inches high. I knew what beets should look like as I saw them freshly displayed in grocery stores and farmers' markets. I fought beet-envy. Seriously. Why couldn't *my* beets look like that? They had been in the ground for months—"How long do beets need to be fully mature?" I wondered. Two to three months seemed to be the consensus with my online searches. With that, I decided to harvest my beets, and I was eager to get them in the kitchen and cook with them. The moment came to pull the beets out of the ground. Much to my disappointment, nothing appeared under the leaves except for a shriveled, thin, one-centimeter-long beet. Mature beets usually have long, beautiful red and green leaves that are six-to-twelve inches long and a bulb between one-to-four inches wide. "Sad" would have been an understatement.

So, naturally, I tried again. But not after wallowing a bit. My husband (who was also developing a green thumb but was much more thorough and methodical in his approach) instructed me to add some supplements to our soil. As a root crop, the bulbs needed a fish fertilizer high in phosphorus and potassium. Although it reeked horribly, I added it to our soil. Yet, I did not see any change, especially in the beet department.

Fast-forward three years later and our family has completely redone our backyard. We used to have a grass hill with a receding hairline of dirt. Over the years, we continued to have poor soil erosion when the SoCal rains would come. We finally decided to put in terraced retaining walls (which would become garden beds), stairs in the middle of the yard, and some grass. The backyard got an overhaul. We were also in the midst of God calling us to start a kingdom community house church out of our home. We felt the desire and vision to turn our backyard into a place of hospitality that fostered community.

In the August heat, under the scorching SoCal sun, we decided to demo our old raised garden beds of ten years and move the annual plants to the big, new garden beds. We had only ranunculus corms and dahlia bulbs that we needed to replant since they are annuals. We eagerly (and carefully) dug them up and brought them to the new garden beds housed in the terraces. My research-loving husband found and delivered the perfect gardening soil for our garden beds (a 70/30 mix of sandy loam and compost). We planted the corms and bulbs on the top row garden bed for full visual effect, excited for them to bloom in the spring.

Within the next couple of weeks, we witnessed a fantastic sight: the ranunculus started to bloom (in late August)! Ranunculus are spring annuals, so they typically bloom from March to May, depending on the growing zone. It was unimaginable for them to start sending out their tender shoots during the hottest time of the year. Yet it was happening. A botanic miracle was taking place in our backyard.

A ranunculus bloom in our new garden beds.

It was at that moment that I had a revelation.

The difference was the soil!

Despite the ongoing one-hundred-degree temperatures that SoCal typically experiences in August, these delicate spring flowers were collectively sighing their thanks for being planted in rich, living soil with bioavailable nutrients to make them thrive. I had been trying to grow mature beets, other vegetables, and flowers in weak, shallow soil. When we transplanted the seeds and bulbs, they thrived in the deep, living, rich soil.

This says something about the profound importance of soil. One would think, "Isn't soil just dirt? What's the difference?" It turns out there is a *huge* difference.

Soil. AKA dirt. Why write a book about soil, one of the most common substances on planet Earth? It is a hidden place that life springs from. Some soil is fertile; some is not. The growth of a plant depends on the presence of bioavailable nutrients in the soil and the soil's ability to supply water to the plant. Soil is the unsung hero of our physical health. The health of the food we eat is connected to the health of the soil it grows in. There's also a deep connection between soil and the condition of our spiritual hearts, but I'm getting ahead of myself.

There is a chasm between surviving and thriving. And it all has to do with the soil.

But, as I discovered, I'm not the only one who knows this.

2

The Lay of the Land

THE BIBLE WAS WRITTEN in an agrarian society, "agrarian" meaning the community's economy was driven by crop production and farmland maintenance. Simply put, without access to today's technology, most people throughout the millennia were involved with farming. As such, *everyone* was intimately familiar with farming when the Bible was written. Farming wasn't a hobby; it was survival. The Bible is filled with examples of farming, sowing, and harvesting.

Jesus, who grew up during this agrarian period (and is the Creator of all things), knew His audience and followers. The Gospels of Matthew, Mark, and Luke[1] all record Jesus sharing a parable illustrating the importance of the state and health of the soil, equating soil to the condition of our hearts.

This parable, sometimes referred to as the Parable of the Sower (AKA "The Four Soils"), is where the focus of this book resides:

> That same day Jesus went out of the house and sat by the lake. Such large crowds gathered around him that he got into a boat and sat in it, while all the people stood on the shore. Then he told them many things in

1. This parable is found in Matt 13, Mark 4, and Luke 8, but we will focus on Matt 13 for the duration of this book.

parables, saying: "A farmer went out to sow his seed. As he was scattering the seed, some fell along the path, and the birds came and ate it up. Some fell on rocky places, where it did not have much soil. It sprang up quickly, because the soil was shallow. But when the sun came up, the plants were scorched, and they withered because they had no root. Other seed fell among thorns, which grew up and choked the plants. Still other seed fell on good soil, where it produced a crop—a hundred, sixty or thirty times what was sown. Whoever has ears, let them hear." (Matt 13: 1–9)[2]

And, because I have a high affection for the Message paraphrase, here is this passage, paraphrased:

"What do you make of this? A farmer planted seed. As he scattered the seed, some of it fell on the road, and birds ate it. Some fell in the gravel; it sprouted quickly but didn't put down roots, so when the sun came up it withered just as quickly. Some fell in the weeds; as it came up, it was strangled by the weeds. Some fell on good earth, and produced a harvest beyond his wildest dreams. Are you listening to this? Really listening?" (Matt 13:3–8)[3]

Dear reader, are you ready to *dig* into this passage? (OK, pun intended.) Let's set our shovels at the top layer and go for it.

IT'S ALL ABOUT THE SOIL

We rely on soil in many ways. In Gen 3:19, God tells Adam and Eve, "By the sweat of your brow you will eat your food until you return to the ground, since from it you were taken; for dust you are and to dust you will return."[4]

What a humbling thing soil/dirt/dust is. We were made from dirt (see Gen 2:7); to dirt we will return when we die. Fun fact, "human" comes from the Latin word "humus," which means "earth" or

2. NIV.

3. MSG.

4. NIV.

"ground." So, we literally came from dirt. We are made up of dirt. Food, the sustenance for our bodies, comes from dirt.

A healthy soil consists of four elements: minerals, organic matter, water, and air. These elements work together to create an environment necessary for seeds to grow.

In the Parable of the Sower, Jesus lays out and establishes the symbolism for us. In this passage, Jesus points out that the farmer is God, the seed is the word of the Kingdom (Matt 13:19)[5], and the soil is the condition of our hearts. And though this first parable of Jesus is named "the parable of the *sower*," I believe Jesus' point is the condition of the *soils*. Put simply, Jesus is telling us that the state of our *hearts* matters.

Our hearts.

Let's talk about it.

I believe there is not enough talk today about the condition of our hearts and "keeping our hearts with all diligence" (Prov 4:23). We can easily find more popular advice on the *authority* of our heart than in *keeping* it.

These famous sayings are everywhere:

"Follow your heart; it knows the way."

"Trust yourself."

"Your heart knows the way—run in that direction."

"If it's in your heart, go for it."

While these mantras can sound so appealing and promising (and even true!), they ultimately lead us astray to a dead-end road. When we don't take Prov 4:23 seriously about keeping watch over our hearts, we can easily settle for addressing the symptoms of the issues of life—worry, stress, unforgiveness, envy, depression, etc.—instead of the problem itself. Sadly, we are often OK living life on the exterior, not digging deeper to see what network of lies and unresolved issues lay beneath the surface.

Much of this superficial and supplemental work is being done today, even in the church in the West, even with good intentions. Very little work is lasting, healthy, or getting to the root of the problem. Attending a church service for one hour a week doesn't form you into Christlikeness as much as the other 167 hours in your week. In that hour, it can be challenging to be vulnerable with other believers, have some deep prayer time, etc. For example, I was a Christian for about twenty years before I more fully understood the Holy Spirit and his role in my salvation, sanctification, and life. I didn't understand the absolute importance of the skill of repentance, or the nature of the enemy of my soul and his plan to take me out, or the authority God has given me as His daughter to walk with Him in freedom. How is that possible? I get a righteous anger when I think about these things and I am desperate to partner with the Lord in helping Christians learn these skills and truths early on in their walk with God.

I am *so* thankful for my Baptist background, where I gained a solid understanding of the Bible. But God, in His mercy, opened my eyes through various events and connections to understand the person of the Holy Spirit. He is our Helper, Counselor, Teacher, and Advocate (John 16:7). Instead of becoming a Christian and trying to be good on our own, we have the Holy Spirit to help us and guide us and do the deep work in our lives.

Keeping things at surface-level isn't what God created us for. Strikingly, the same can be said of the condition of our physical soil and its management and stewardship, especially here in the West and its modern farming practices. There is a difference between modern farming and sustainable agriculture.

A short explanation: modern farming relies heavily upon pesticides and antibiotics to produce heavy crops, using the least amount of inputs. On the other hand, sustainable agriculture relies on good stewarding and activating the natural systems and resources on the farm. Over time, modern farming does violence to the soil where outside resources are required to continue farming while sustainable agriculture implements a cycle of renewable health and richness. Here is the connection I discovered as I began to garden:

There are strong parallels between the health of our heart and the health of actual soil.

Hang with me a bit more as I geek out on gardening wisdom. I promise it ties into everything here.

As with physical soil, if the soil of our heart is anemic, hard, poison drenched, artificially supplemented, and dry, the crop or fruit produced will match it (*if* any crop emerges and survives). Contrast this toxic soil with soil that is rich, living, biodiverse, free of weeds and pests, teeming with life from organic matter that has been redeemed, well watered, soft, and free of pesticides and artificial supplements, and the seed will thrive and produce a bountiful crop.

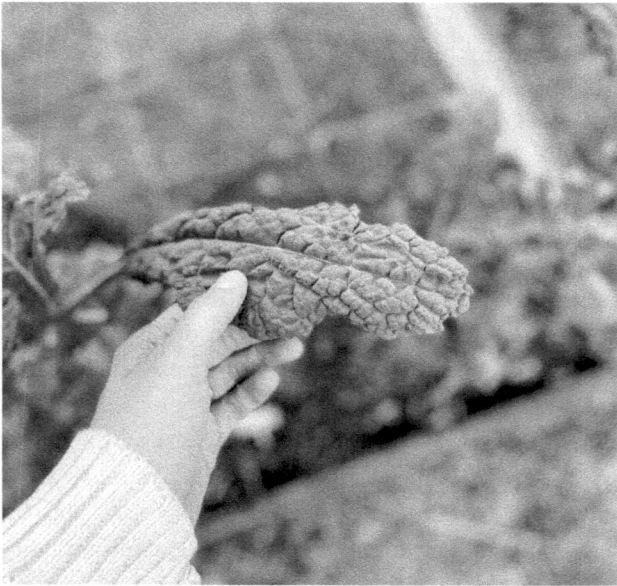

"Living soil" is a gardening method centered on microbial life inside the soil. Scientists are finding a symbiotic relationship between the plants and the microbial life in the soil: fungi, protozoa, and other types.[6] "Living" soil means that the soil's microbiome is healthy and well balanced with needed nutrients, good drainage, and active microbiology and biodiversity, often including worms,

6. Jacoby et al., "Role of Soil Microorganisms."

fungi, and other healthy bacteria. To put it plainly, living soil is soil that eats and feeds. It's essentially a mini ecosystem.

One could summarize this soil/life relationship:

Healthy Soil = Healthy Crops; Unhealthy Soil = Unhealthy Crops.

A popular saying in the gardening world is, "You are feeding the soil, not the plant!" Creating living soil is achieved by building the soil, meaning you spend your efforts nourishing the microbes, insects, worms, etc. It's not using isolated nutrients in a bottle from Home Depot but feeding the soil to ensure all nutrients are bio-available when your plant needs them.

What are some things that benefit the health of the soil? Sunlight, sufficient water, nutrients, no crowding of thorns and weeds, and organic matter (dead leaves, animal waste, etc.).

What are some things that lead to positive heart change? God's grace and grace from others; community; time in God's Word (soaking in truth); positive boundaries or lack thereof; a biblical understanding of our enemy; a habit and love for repentance; time in God's presence; prayer; and space and margin to grow.

Living soil aims to have rich soil on which the seed falls, takes root, and produces a fruitful crop. Similarly, the goal in our lives should be to cultivate good hearts on which we receive the word of the Kingdom (the seeds), and the seeds take root and bear much fruit for the Kingdom. It is from there that we become true disciples and produce fruit to the glory of God and for the good of those around us, as Matt 13:8 tells us: "Still other seed fell on good soil, where it produced a crop—a hundred, sixty or thirty times what was sown."[7]

THE HEART OF THE MATTER (HEARTS 101)

Jesus had much to say about our hearts. He said, "For where your treasure is, there your heart will be also." (Matt 6:21).[8] In the Old

7. NIV.
8. NIV.

Testament, Solomon wisely said in Prov 27:19, "As water reflects the face, so one's life reflects the heart."[9] If our hearts carry so much weight, we must put effort into caring for them. Saint Augustine wrote between AD 397 and 400, "Where your pleasure is, there is your treasure; where your treasure is, there is your heart; where your heart is, there is your happiness."[10]

The author of Proverbs warns in Prov 4:23, "Above all else, guard your heart, for everything you do flows from it."[11]

The Message paraphrase says, "Keep vigilant watch over your heart; *that's* where life starts" (Prov 4:23).[12]

"Above everything else, guard your heart; for it is the source of life's consequences."[13]

"Keep your heart with all vigilance, for from it flow the springs of life."[14]

Scripture teaches that the state of our hearts is our responsibility. Let that sink in for a moment. Wait, what? Is my heart *my* responsibility? Yup. That's what Scripture says. Our hearts are *ours* to guard, protect, defend, watch over, and keep an eye on. Our lives are a reflection of what is going on in our hearts.

But is my heart completely *my* responsibility? I'm so glad you asked! That question likely spurs additional questions. You may ask, "Am I solely responsible for my heart? Or are the people around me, and God, responsible for it?" Or you may say, "I mean, things have happened to me that have hurt me, or influenced me in ways I didn't want. What do I do with the wrongs done to me in my life that I never asked for? The things I had no control over?"

Yes, those things you went through were hard, and I'm deeply sorry. They happened, and they greatly affected you, and I wish I could give you a big hug! We *all* go through trials and hardships, some more than others, it seems. But leaving those past hurts in

---

9. NIV.

10. Augustine of Hippo Quotes.

11. NIV.

12. MSG; emphasis original.

13. CJB.

14. ESV.

the dark, never bringing them into the open and into the light for God's healing will cause your heart to become a toxic cesspool. Unforgiveness is a poison. Unresolved anger is a poison. Vengeance is a poison. Jealousy is a poison. Your heart is still your responsibility. (And trust me, in writing this book, I have had multiple growing moments in which I am challenged to continue to practice this. I've had to do the hard work of tending to my heart when I've been wronged or perceive being wronged.) It's good *and* hard work, my friends, just like weeding a garden. It's hard work, but so therapeutic, too.

Throughout life, we will experience very difficult things like traumatic events; we may incur deep wounds from a friend; we experience rejection; and we will have opportunities to extend forgiveness. We have to understand that any of these things, left unresolved in our heart, is an open doorway for Satan to get a foothold in our lives. If you are a follower of Jesus, he is set against you to destroy you. John 10:10 tells us that "the thief comes only to steal and kill and destroy."[15] He's on a mission, and he's looking for an "in." This is why God has instructed us to watch diligently over our hearts.

Graciously, God has given us a skill to fight back for freedom—*repentance*. I will touch more on repentance in a later chapter. But for now, please understand that submitting to God, confessing our sin to Him and others, commanding the enemy to flee from us, and asking the Holy Spirit to dwell in those empty places is the (basic) way to keeping a healthy heart.

Notable people from every walk of life see unforgiveness as the toxic sludge it is. I recently watched a video in which Hollywood actor Jim Carrey professed belief in the forgiveness and grace that Jesus offers. Carrey shared that unforgiveness had become a poison in his soul, and Jesus had freed him from it. Sadly, though, toward the end of his speech, Carrey blended in some empty new age beliefs. But I believe he got the first part right. Carrey understood that unforgiveness is a deadly poison.[16]

15. NIV.
16. Papa, "Jim Carrey."

All of these "poisons" to our hearts start off as a single thought. Often, it is a lie or an idea that we want to believe because it justifies our sin. Most people won't believe an outright lie; they're too easy to spot. It's the lies that are laced with a bit of truth that make it more appealing to swallow. But when we believe a lie and it takes root in our hearts, it grows like a weed as we continue to feed it. We gotta yank that baby! See 2 Cor 10:5: "We take captive every thought to make it obedient to Christ."[17]

Have you seen the goathead weed? In Southern California, where I live, goatheads (also known as puncturevine) are a common nuisance. The hallmark of this hellish weed is the dried seeds which become a multi-thorned, tire-popping, foot-poking menace whose thorns resemble a goat's horns. The other fiendish thing about goatheads is the way the weed grows. Instead of growing vertically like most weeds do, goatheads grow horizontally like a flat carpet, thereby maximizing the area for unsuspecting passersby to get a thorn in the foot, paw, or tire. The seeds can last up to seven years and the plant is drought tolerant. It's pretty hard to get rid of them. They even look demonic. Google it.

Lies that we believe can grow like these goatheads. Little weeds, if not caught early on after they sprout, grow into big weeds. We've had our fair share on our little farm. Especially in the spring, when the meager winter rains have come and gone, our orchard and garden begin to be overtaken by them. We have learned to act quickly once we see little weeds sprouting. It doesn't take much water to get weeds to grow.

17. NIV.

Weeding the garden.

If left long enough, a weed's roots become deeply embedded in the soil, making them impossible for one person to pull out. Sometimes we have spiritual/emotional "weeds" in our lives that we need help pulling out, roots and all. God gives us a weed-busting plan in Jas 5:13–16:[18]

> Is anyone among you in trouble? Let them pray. Is anyone happy? Let them sing songs of praise. Is anyone among you sick? Let them call the elders of the church to pray over them and anoint them with oil in the name of the Lord. And the prayer offered in faith will make the sick person well; the Lord will raise them up. If they have

18. NIV.

sinned, they will be forgiven. Therefore confess your sins to each other and pray for each other so that you may be healed. The prayer of a righteous person is powerful and effective.

When left to grow, weeds eventually produce seeds, generating more seeds to disperse and grow next year. The plant is doing its main job of reproducing and spreading! This parallels how our unconfessed sins greatly affect the people around us. Hebrews 12:15 tells us, "See to it that no one falls short of the grace of God and that no bitter root grows up to cause trouble and defile many."[19] What do you want growing in your heart?

Allow me to share another garden story to illustrate this truth for you with two words: nut grass. Nut grass (also known as nutsedge) gets its name from the nutlets that grow underground that feed the blades of grass it sends up out of the soil. In SoCal, this grass is a devilish and invasive weed that garden experts have dubbed "one of the worst weeds," as they are one of the most hated weeds by gardeners.[20]

A year after getting our new soil into the new garden beds, we left for a glorious five-week road trip vacation. Upon our return, we saw our virgin garden beds covered in this long-flowing beach type of grass. There was *so* much. Out of nowhere. But we didn't act right away. The school year commenced upon our return, and life, as expected, got busy.

Fast-forward five months from then when we started to plan our spring and summer garden. My amazing, green-thumbed gardener husband did the research, and we *had* to pull out all of the nut grass repeatedly over four months (and currently still going . . .). With this beast of a weed, it doesn't die until you've either removed all of the nutlets that are in a complex network six inches underground or you've starved the nuts by plucking the grass repeatedly. We can't spray it because the specialized herbicide will remain in the garden bed and lace our precious veggies with poison.

---

19. NIV.
20. Ramirez, "Nut Grass."

So, we spent the next several months pulling out nut grass as a family. If that isn't a practical lesson of not letting sin fester in our lives, kids, I don't know what is! Nut grass will not go away until the root is pulled and/or the grass is starved. It *must* be dealt with. Ignoring this weed would have adverse consequences to our newly planted vegetables and herbs during the coming years.

OK, moving on from nut grass! The point is that weeds can take up valuable real estate in the garden bed or orchard. Weeds use up precious nutrients in the soil that could be used for crops. Weeds compete with our desired plants for needed space and sunlight. In short, the gardener must stay on top of the weeds if they want a fruitful garden.

Friend, *you* are the guard of your garden (heart)! What will you allow to be planted, watered, and grown in your heart?

Interestingly, Scripture clearly tells us that our heart and our thoughts are inseparable. Proverbs 23:7 tells us, "For as [a man] thinks in his heart, so is he."[21] Now, in context, that verse is referring to the verse before it, giving an example that a miser will do what a miser thinks he is in his heart. To put it simply, our thoughts become us.

There's a beautiful poem penned by Ralph Waldo Emerson that author and teacher John Mark Comer calls "a working theory of the law of returns applied to spiritual formation."[22] Emerson puts it simply and succinctly:

> Sow a thought and you reap an action;
> Sow an act and you reap a habit;
> Sow a habit and you reap a character;
> Sow a character and you reap a destiny.

So, you may think, this is all great and resonates with me, but how do I practically keep watch over my heart? Glad you asked. Turn the page.

---

21. AMP.
22. Comer, *Live No Lies*, 189.

3

Jesus, the Master Gardener

THE HOW

So, what is good heart-soil, and how do we cultivate it and keep watch over our hearts? Just like with gardening, tending to our hearts takes time and intentionality. The goal of the "garden of your heart" is for it to be so healthy that much fruit is produced from it, for the glory of God and the good of others, as one wonderful church body says it.[1]

First, it takes time. Good heart-soil is cultivated over time. It doesn't take place at the speed of a microwave or a freeway. It requires a commitment to intentional attention and rhythms for rich, living soil to develop. Days, months, years. As needed elements are added to it (called an "amendment"), the soil becomes richer. An amendment is any material added to the soil to improve its physical or chemical properties.[2]

Second, cultivating soil requires intentionality. A gardener must be intentional about maintaining the health of the soil.

1. South Beach Church Slogan.
2. "Cornell CALS."

Amending the soil takes time. It takes time to break down organic matter to make it bioavailable to any plants. To cultivate anything in our lives takes attention, resources, time, and action. Proverbs 21:5 tells us, "The plans of the diligent lead surely to abundance."[3] Being diligent is to be intentional. Things don't get done without intentionality.

Now, let's get to how this relates to our hearts. In Matt 13:18–23, the word that Jesus used for the heart is καρδια (*kardia*—kardee'-ah). Interestingly, this word does not refer to the physical, beating heart inside our human bodies. It's not a heart in the sense of romance or of Hallmark movies.[4] In the Bible, the Hebrew and Greek languages map out the heart as the whole person—our mind, will, and emotions. It's made up of the core of who we are, including our thoughts.

Our whole person.

Not compartmentalized.

It's integrated.

Congruent.

Whole.

It takes intentionality to care for our hearts, like working through hurts and misunderstandings and intentionally working toward a "whole" heart. Working through hardships in life takes time, and figuring out where to spend our time and attention takes time and thought.

Just hearing that we need to be fruitful doesn't just magically make it happen. We can easily be hearers of the word, but not understand it. It takes intentionality and even wrestling to understand something, especially something of great value.

Going forward, Matt 13:23 says, "But the seed falling on good soil refers to someone who hears the word and *understands* it. This is the one who produces a crop, yielding a hundred, sixty or thirty times what was sown."[5] The Greek word for "understand" here is συνίημι (*syniēmi*, soon-ee'-ay-mee), which means "to

3. ESV.

4. RJM, "Matthew 13:1–9; 18–23."

5. NIV.

consider, understand, be wise, to put together, i.e., (mentally) to comprehend."[6]

Jesus is the one who sows the seed many times—and extravagantly—even in seemingly careless places! He sows the seed in hope that the soil it lands on is fertile, deep; that we may repent, be healed by Him, and bear much fruit.

Let's take a closer look at the types of soils Jesus described in His parable and start making the connection between the soils and our hearts.

TYPES OF SOILS

In Matt 13:18–23,[7] Jesus lays out for us four types of soil on which the farmer scattered and sowed his seed:

> Listen then to what the parable of the sower means: When anyone hears the message about the kingdom and does not understand it, the evil one comes and snatches away what was sown in their heart. This is the seed sown along the path. The seed falling on rocky ground refers to someone who hears the word and at once receives it with joy. But since they have no roots, they last only a short time. When trouble or persecution comes because of the word, they quickly fall away. The seed falling among the thorns refers to someone who hears the word, but the worries of this life and the deceitfulness of wealth choke the word, making it unfruitful. But the seed falling on good soil refers to someone who hears the word and understands it. This is the one who produces a crop, yielding a hundred, sixty or thirty times what was sown.

Now in the Message paraphrase:

> Study this story of the farmer planting seed. When anyone hears news of the kingdom and doesn't take it in, it just remains on the surface, and so the Evil One comes along and plucks it right out of that person's heart. This is

6. "Matt 13:23 Translation and Meaning."

7. NIV.

the seed the farmer scatters on the road. The seed cast in the gravel—this is the person who hears and instantly responds with enthusiasm. But there is no soil of character, and so when the emotions wear off and some difficulty arrives, there is nothing to show for it. The seed cast in the weeds is the person who hears the kingdom news, but weeds of worry and illusions about getting more and wanting everything under the sun strangle what was heard, and nothing comes of it. The seed cast on good earth is the person who hears and takes in the News, and then produces a harvest beyond his wildest dreams.

Let's break it down:

Fell Along the Path

Birds came and ate it up (Satan is always at the ready to snatch away the word).

Rocky Places

Not much soil; the plants sprang up quickly but withered when the sun came up because they had no root (shallow soil; the plants didn't have to work hard to connect to a water source). When trouble or persecution comes because of the word, they quickly fall away.

Fell Among Thorns

The thorns grew up and choked the plants. Some are faced with the danger of riches.[8] The worries of this life, the deceitfulness of wealth, and the desires for other things come in and choke the word, making it unfruitful. This happens too often and easily with genuine followers.

Fell on Good Soil

It produced a crop (one hundred, sixty, or thirty times what was sown)—if we can assume that there is healthy soil and roots and that it is free of thorns and weeds.

Let's take a closer look at each one:

8. "Words of Life Ministries."

1. The Seed that Fell Along the Path/Hard Ground

This person hears the news about the Kingdom of God but does not understand it. This seed is vulnerable and susceptible on the hard ground, and therefore, Satan can come and snatch away what was sown in their heart. This soil (heart) is hard and neglected. It has likely been trodden over many times and is now hard. This heart is unaffected by the word and it is inattentive. It likely has no framework for the good news. It is most likely not open to receiving the word, where the word just sits on the heart but does not get *in* the heart. Maybe it has put up walls in the past because of hurts and wrongs done to it.

2. Fell on Rocky Places

This is someone who receives the word at once with joy, but because they have no root in the shallow soil, when persecution or troubles comes because of the word, they quickly fall away. This could easily be a situation where someone has a conversion experience but is tragically fed a watered-down gospel. There are many reasons a person could fall away from following Jesus. The emphasis here is that there is *no root* because of shallow soil, and their hearts quickly turn away because of persecution due to being a Christian. Perhaps it is a lordship issue and a lack of surrender? A fear-of-God issue? A lack-of-abiding issue? A surface-Christianity issue? The roots *must* go down deep!

This is something I am super passionate about and was just talking to our kids about during our morning devotion time today. We can know so much about God, have many Bible verses memorized, but that is surface-level Christianity. If we don't *know* God personally, spend time with Him in His presence, encountering Him, it is much easier to fall away when things get hard. Our roots go down deep in God's marvelous love by spending the time cultivating relationship with Him in prayer and in worship and in His Word.

I used this example for my kids to understand this: say I really wanted you to know my friend Ashley. I would tell you all about her. I would tell you that she has blonde hair, is five-foot-six, athletic, thoughtful, fun, talented at making charcuterie boards, and loves God. I could describe her until you had everything memorized about who my friend Ashley is. But, you've still not met her. You've not been in her presence. So, you can't say that you know her, because you don't. You only know facts *about* her.

Friends, this is what I'm talking about. We must *know* God! He aches to have that relationship and connection with you. He's waiting. Why don't you take a moment right now and open up a conversation with Him and sing your favorite worship song to Him, just because? Go ahead. This book can wait!

One last root issue I feel compelled to talk about is this: maybe it's a post-COVID-not-going-to-church-but-watching-the-livestream issue? That last one was hard to type, but I believe it needs to be said in complete love.

If you are one of these Christians, with much grace and truth, I urge you to get connected to a local body of believers. Find a vibrant and alive church congregation or a sound house church—Spirit-filled and grounded in Scripture—and get connected into a community with other Christians. Watching a livestream while isolated at home is putting yourself in a very vulnerable position. Just as a pack of wolves knows that they'll win a lunch if they can get a sheep isolated from the rest of the herd, so Christians fall prey to the devil and his schemes to steal, kill, and destroy (John 10:10)[9] when they give up gathering together (Heb 10:25).[10]

This shallow-soil Christianity needs an infusion of community to be able to withstand the "heat" of persecution which will happen if they're following Jesus.

9. NIV.
10. NIV.

3. Fell Among Thorns

This is someone who hears the word but is double-minded and preoccupied with the worries of this life and the deceitfulness of wealth. It chokes the word, making it unfruitful (Gen 3).

Boy, is this a word for our generation. Preoccupied much? Distracted much? Struggling with materialism? Trying to juggle it all? Trying to hear God in the midst of the incessant noise?

This is the soil that I personally struggle with the most. I have seasons where my life is more like good soil (obviously not ever perfect), but if I'm not in that category, this is where I fall.

Living in the twenty-first century comes with both its perks and its challenges. Most of us aren't preoccupied on a moment-to-moment basis about our physical survival, as many of our ancestors had to be. We now have clean, running water, dishwashers, cars, varied types of technology, you name it. So many luxuries that we forget they are luxuries. In 2007, though, our world changed in a big way with the invention of the iPhone.

The iPhone has shrunken our attention spans, introduced an exponential amount of distractions to our already overloaded brains and schedules, and it has brought with it an overall misguided feeling of omnipresence, which, I would argue, is detrimental to our hearts. Let's go back to the text, though.

It says that the one who received this seed is preoccupied with "the worries of this world, and the deceitfulness of wealth *chokes* the word and makes it unfruitful." Have you seen this to be true in your life? When your schedule is packed, or you're distracted with your phone or to do list, are you seeking the Kingdom of God and abiding in Jesus? I find it hard to let the fruit of the Spirit ooze out of my pores when I'm living this way. If you answered "yes," please come and teach me how you do it.

Really, the answer is "no!" No, we can't live lives in constant communion with God when we're continually distracted and pulled in multiple directions. John Mark Comer summed it up best in his amazing book *The Ruthless Elimination of Hurry*: "Hurry and love are incompatible."[11]

Furthermore, Corrie Ten Boom said, "Both sin and busyness have the exact same effect—they cut off our connection to God, to other people, and even to our own soul."[12]

I find it interesting that the action that happens to the seed's fruit is "choke." Let's tease out the definition of "choke" a bit, shall we? To "choke" means to "have severe difficulty in breathing because of a constricted or obstructed throat or lack of air." It's cutting off the air supply that is necessary for life. It makes my soul shiver to picture a tomato plant that has sprouted from a seed and was supposed to bloom and produce many tomatoes throughout the summer, but something comes and literally chokes it, and over a couple of days, it dies because it was obstructed from receiving life. Ugh! Can you picture it? Not a pretty picture. I don't know about you, but it doesn't take more than a day of me not staying connected with the Vine (Jesus) throughout my day in His Word and prayer for me to start to feel like I'm suffocating. I bet I'm not alone.

4. Fell on Good Soil

Ah, the soil we long to be. This is someone who hears the word and understands it. (There's that word "understanding" again!) This person is receptive, open, humble and surrendered. This is the one who will produce a crop one hundred, sixty, or thirty times what was sown.

In order for a seed to become fruitful, it needs healthy, tilled, and deep soil; adequate water; plenty of sunshine; and shelter as it is first sprouting up out of the ground.

---

11. Comer, *Ruthless Elimination*, 23.
12. Quoted in Comer, *Ruthless Elimination*, 20.

Fruitful spaghetti squash harvest.

WHAT'S THE DIFFERENCE?

So, you may wonder, what's the main difference between the three infertile soils and the one fertile soil? There's a very crucial word that Jesus repeated in so many of His parables. *The word is* "understand."

Many times we read, "Whoever has ears, let them *hear*" (Matt 13:9).[13] In verse 19, He says, "When anyone *hears* the

13. NIV; emphasis mine.

message about the Kingdom and does not understand it . . ." So, we can gather from this that it is very possible to hear Jesus's words but actually not understand them. I don't know about you, but that scares me a bit. I don't want to miss what Jesus is saying here.

Understanding requires a deeper action than hearing. The magic ingredient is:

trust

The natural progression God desires is *hear, understand, act/ obey* (coming from trust!). For example, when I give one of my children an instruction, they hear it, but they must also have the understanding to act. There's a jump that happens between hearing and understanding. God's been after our trust since He put the two trees in the garden and told us not to eat from the tree of the knowledge of good and evil. He knows that trust is everything in relationships.

It is the same here.

Here's what Jesus said to explain this further:

> He [Jesus] replied, "Because the knowledge of the secrets of the kingdom of heaven has been given to you, but not to them. Whoever has will be given more, and they will have an abundance. Whoever does not have, even what they have will be taken from them. This is why I speak to them in parables: Though seeing, they do not see; though hearing, they do not hear or understand. In them is fulfilled the prophecy of Isaiah: You will be ever hearing but never understanding; you will be ever seeing but never perceiving. For this people's heart has become calloused; they hardly hear with their ears, and they have closed their eyes. Otherwise they might see with their eyes, hear with their ears, understand with their hearts and turn, and I would heal them (Matt 13:11–15).[14]

The Message paraphrase says it beautifully:

> "He [Jesus] replied, "You've [the disciples] been given insight into God's kingdom. You know how it works. Not

14. NIV.

everybody has this gift, this insight; it hasn't been given to them. Whenever someone has a ready, trusting heart for this, the insights and understandings flow freely. But if there is no readiness or trust, any trace of receptivity soon disappears. That's why I tell stories: to create readiness, to nudge the people toward a welcome awakening. In their present state they can stare till doomsday and not see it, listen till they're blue in the face and not get it. I don't want Isaiah's forecast repeated all over again: Your ears are open but you don't hear a thing. Your eyes are awake but you don't see a thing. The people are stupid! They stick fingers in their ears so they won't have to listen; they screw their eyes shut so they won't have to look, so they won't have to deal with me face-to-face and let me heal them" (Matt 13:11–14).[15]

Jesus is telling us that we must pay attention to what we hear, to lean in close to *His* voice and teachings, not ignore Him, and then act in trust. In our lives, we will hear millions of things said to us. Our "soil" is determined by what we allow ourselves to truly hear, understand, absorb, and act upon. Remember, we are the guardians of our hearts, and we must guard it for the glory of God.

So, we must ask ourselves—what kind of hearers are we?[16] Are you a distracted hearer because of the hundreds of Instagram posts your mind imbibes and marinates in during the day? Or are you a defiant hearer who has hurt and unforgiveness in your heart, so you don't want to listen? Or are you tuned in, as a desired radio channel, where God's voice is clear and static-free? We must keep our attention sharp to God's voice. Love is the giving of attention. But don't miss the last part about hearing and understanding: when we hear God's word, we must combine it with trust and then act accordingly.

Here is one of my main points:

Our hearts need to be prepared to receive the word of God.

Just as farmers till and prepare their soil before sowing seed, so must we pray for our heart to be open and "tilled" before the

---

15. MSG; added words mine.
16. "Study 1 The Farmer, the Seed, and the Soils."

Lord, just as we pray for others to be ready to hear the word. We do this through *prayer*. Prayer is what tills up the soil in hearts. We do this regularly with our kids during our family devotion time. We need to take time to till our hearts before Him so we are receptive to His Word.

God tells us to do this in Hos 10:12! Hosea the prophet is calling Israel to repent and seek Him:

> Sow righteousness for yourselves, reap the fruit of unfailing love, and break up your unplowed ground; for it is time to seek the LORD, until he comes and showers his righteousness on you.[17]

We who are preachers and teachers must remember this. Prayer is vital in the ministry that God has given you in preaching the Word of God. Prayer will get the soil ready for hearts to receive the Word when you teach. Otherwise, it can fall on deaf ears and be unfruitful. This goes for our families, too. If we do a good job reading the Bible every day as a family but we're not praying for our kids' hearts to be "good soil hearts" and teaching them this, then it very likely could be unfruitful.

What a difference prayer makes! I am preaching this to my heart as much as yours, dear friend. I've gone through times of spending more time in prayer, but prayer doesn't always come "easy" to me (whatever that means!). What I mean by that is that it is a struggle for me to stay consistent in praying often. But I will say, the most "successful" way I've had in praying is praying as I go about my day. Like practicing the presence of God in the everyday moments of life. Talking to Jesus as a friend. Sharing my heart with Him, listening to His. The best book I would recommend on learning about prayer is Tyler Staton's *Praying Like Monks, Living Like Fools.*

Don't get discouraged, teachers, if the results seem small. There will always be the four types of hearers/soils. We are to do the work of tilling/praying, and He sows the seed/the Word. Our responsibility does not ultimately lie with how people receive it.

17. NIV.

With good soil hearts, Jesus has this to say: "If you hold to my teaching, you are really my disciples" (John 8:31).[18] We are to be deeply rooted in the Word and hold tight to it.

WORD OF ENCOURAGEMENT TO PARENTS

As a parent, I've experienced more than ever the truth of Prov 18:21—"Death and life are in the power of the tongue, and those who love it and indulge it will eat its fruit and bear the consequences of their words"[19]. As parents, we have so much influence on our children's hearts, for good or for bad. So much of that influence comes from how we live our lives, and the words we choose to say, and *how* we say them to our children.

I'd bet that you desire to be a good parent. You want to give your child a firm foundation of faith, good character, work ethic, and healthy relationships. Kudos, and I applaud you!

But parents, we must first pay attention to our soil (our heart).

Is *our* heart muddled up with unforgiveness, sin and compromise with the world, no margin, or a lack of rootedness in God? Those closest to us will be directly impacted, which, for parents, that's our kids. They're our closest neighbors. Our hearts greatly affect those around us, especially the closest ones.

As a parent, we must "keep our heart with all vigilance, for from it flow the springs of life" (Prov 4:23[20]). If we don't, disease will start leaking out of our soil, our heart. Trust me, I know from experience. Unchecked and unprocessed emotions, thoughts, etc., poison our hearts.

It's like the oxygen mask routine on airplanes. Parents are instructed to first secure their own oxygen mask so they can then turn around and secure their child's. I remember when I was younger, that seemed so backwards, even unfair! Shouldn't the children be attended to first? In a way, yes, actually. A big way that

18. NIV.
19. AMP.
20. ESV.

we make our children's lives a priority in ours is by taking care of ourselves first. It's not selfish, it's vital. (I'm still learning this. . .)

I remember hearing a woman speak at a MOPS gathering when I was a new mom to our 3-month old. She is a counselor, and has a warm and lovingly firm demeanor. I've never forgotten what she said about motherhood, "If I could go back to the beginning of motherhood with my 3 girls, I would have focused more on working on myself, my walk with God, and my issues so I could have been an even better mom." Wow. And this woman did motherhood beautifully, from what I knew, and have continued to see, as she is now a grandmother.

But it's true. We will all have regrets; goodness, I already do, being only 15 years into my journey of parenthood. I wish I could rewind time so I could have entered into the 4th sibling squabble of the day with rootedness in Jesus, which would mean patience and empathy springing forth, instead of fear, then it's close relative, anger. "Hindsight is always 20/20," they say.

If we understand this truth about tending to our soil/heart, it will deeply impact our children, too. Cultivating a good soil heart will bring a legacy for our children to follow. We have to show our kids how to watch over their hearts with all diligence, especially in this time of cultural identity confusion, constant voices speaking ideas to us, distractions, false teachings, technology, and all of the messages that come with it. As John Mark Comer quotes, "As Willard once said, "We truly live at the mercy of our ideas.."[21]

---

21. Comer, *Live No Lies*, 27.

4

Tending to Your Heart
(and Garden)

IN GARDENING, THE FIRST step in amending soil is to evaluate it.
Study it. Find out where it is lacking and what it needs. In tending
to our hearts, the first step in cultivating a resilient and surrendered heart is to sit with God and ask Him to search our heart
(Ps 139:23–24).[1] Amendments bring health to soil that is in need
of change. If you have healthy soil, you'll have a healthy, nutrient-
dense crop! In short, what crops eat directly impacts our nutrition
as humans. "Fertilizers improve the supply of nutrients in the soil,
directly affecting plant growth. Soil amendments improve a soil's
physical condition (e.g., soil structure, water infiltration), indirectly affecting plant growth."[2] Our soil is so diverse—the microbiome
in our gut is more delicate and diverse than all the species in the
rainforest.[3] Fascinatingly, scientists are seeing a strong connection
between the soil microbiome and the microbiome of our guts.[4]

---

1. NIV.

2 University of California Agriculture & Natural Resources, "Fertilizers
vs. Soil Amendments."

3. Dirt to Dinner.

4. "Healthy Soil."

This means that what is in the soil goes into our food, which goes into our bodies. Interesting connection?

AMENDMENT OF WATER
(GRACE)

Have you ever been to a desert? Have you walked over those cracked, puzzle-like pieces of dried, parched dirt? We all know that deserts are the way they are because of the very limited amount of rain that falls in that type of climate and biome. Without water, soil becomes hardened. Interestingly, after a desert has a good rainfall, the soil has a hard time retaining the water, and flooding occurs! The soil has been hardened by the sun and stripped of all of its moisture, which makes it hard to accept and absorb water when it does come. There's a term to describe this. "Hydrophobic" (break it down—hydro [water] + phobic [fear]) means that super dry soil automatically wants to shed water, so you have to give it two to three waterings before planting anything.

Soil also becomes hardened when it is trampled repeatedly by man or animal. Another word for this is "compaction." When soil is compacted, all of the air is pressed out of the soil by stress. This reduces pore space between the particles of the soil. Compacted soil reduces the effectiveness of water infiltration and drainage.

Our hearts can become hardened and dry. This happens through many different things. Disobedience. Idolatry. Ignoring the promptings of the Holy Spirit. Walking in the flesh, not the Spirit. Unforgiveness. Lack of repentance. Sin committed against us. Unresolved hurt. Believing and living lies.

What is the one thing that can cure hardened soil? *Water.*

What is the one thing that can cure a hardened heart? *Grace.*

Human beings cannot thrive without grace. We need grace from God. We need grace in relationships. We need grace for ourselves. Like drinking water throughout our day, we need grace throughout the entirety of our day.

We need grace from God. If you've seen *Les Miserables*, you're aware of the opening scene where Jean Valjean (an escaped convict) is invited to dine and stay at the bishop's house. He accepts the invitation, dines with the bishop and his loving but fretful wife, and is invited to stay the night. During the night, he has a nightmare and wakes up and steals the family's silver. He is caught. But I'm not going to spoil it for you. Find the clip on YouTube[5] and you'll be moved by it far more than my description here. I was going through a life-changing discipleship course called *Story-Formed Life*[6] for the first time during the COVID pandemic. As I watched this clip, it overwhelmed my heart with an understanding of God's grace.

I grew up in a loving, first-generation Christian home. My parents taught me about God and his Son Jesus, and we went to church regularly as a family. At the age of nine, after family devotions, I told my dad one night that I wanted to follow Jesus. We prayed, he explained some truths to me, and I'll never forget that night. I knew that I had decided something big. I remember ending our time together by saying to him, "Daddy, I'm going to be the best Christian ever!" Oh my, dear nine-year-old Michelle. I remember my Dad graciously saying, "Michelle, you're going to have ups and downs in your walk with Christ, but He is faithful." I still remember feeling that I would *still* be the best Christian ever. (Whatever that even means.) I would work hard to do a good job and excel at it. And yes, sadly, I've carried that performance-based identity into my walk with Christ through my forty-two years on this earth, and I've repented of it, though I'm still a work in progress.

Back then, I didn't really understand what God's grace was. I knew the Word and that it was important. It wasn't until the last ten years that I've truly come to understand what grace is, in increasing measure each year as I walk with Jesus.

I'm a firm believer of this fact: *You don't know what grace is until you need it.*

Allow me to share part of my testimony. I was the "good Christian girl" growing up. All the way until my mid-twenties, I

5. Wilson, "Les Miserables."
6. See www.storyformedlife.org.

was always trying to do the right thing: be obedient, not cause any waves, be super conscientious, polite, follow the Bible . . . You get the picture. But, when my husband and I became parents, especially after our second child was born, I found myself getting angry at times. Simple things like spilled milk, another sleepless night up with a teething toddler, or soothing a screaming one-year-old would push me over the edge. I felt frustrated that things weren't going smoothly and somehow I was failing when things went wrong. What was happening to me? It was like an out-of-body experience. I had not struggled with anger all of my life (I am so thankful that I had not experienced any trauma or really difficult things growing up), and now, out of the blue, here I am losing my temper when my one-year-old dumps his snack bowl on the floor intentionally again. I was faced with my sinfulness. I do *not* say this out of a spirit of self-righteousness. In all transparency, I've had to realize it was my Pharisee-like behavior that drove me for years. I wanted to be righteous. I wanted to be a good Christian. But I have come to see that this came at a cost, and I was far from understanding the gospel.

When I found myself sinning repeatedly, I had to come to grips with the fact that I *was* a sinner, desperately in need of this thing I had always heard about: God's grace. But before I came to grips with that, I went down the opposite road: self-condemnation. I got really down on myself and condemned myself for getting frustrated at my child for taking too long to put on their shoes. After I had taken time to analyze what had happened and then promised myself to do better next time, I couldn't understand why I kept sinning. And those surface-level sins started revealing to me the deeper sins: lack of trust in God, idolatry of the heart, disobedience, walking in the flesh. Oy.

I'll never forget the time I was driving our five kids to their hybrid homeschool group one morning. They were arguing about something (my kids are all big verbal processors and therefore there's a lot of talking and debating going on in our home), and it got to my last nerve. In the car, I immaturely yelled, "Kids! Please stop your fighting! It accomplishes nothing and brings chaos."

The kids quieted down, but then I was left with my condemnation. How could I yell again when I had promised myself that I wouldn't anymore, that I would take a calmer approach next time? Ugh. And I prayed. I prayed in my driver's seat by the Target intersection, "God, *please* help me! I'm so sick of struggling with this. Please take it away and change me!"

And, immediately after I prayed, I heard God say to my heart so clearly, in a gentle, non-condemning tone:

"Michelle, why are you so focused on this sin?"

I literally jumped in my seat a bit. God spoke back to me, and at first I couldn't believe it was Him—it was just so clear and out of the blue! But He spoke right to my heart. He knew what I needed to hear. God was pointing out that I was so focused on my self-righteousness and my performance. I was thinking too much about how I was doing.

But He showed me that as long as I am focused on *not* sinning, I am majorly missing the point! I was in the business of what people call "sin management." But Jesus came to give me *life*, and life to the full (John 10:10), not just manage my sin and try to be a good girl. Oh, dear friend, Jesus came for much, *much* more than that.

Jesus died for my sins, and yours. He died because He knew I was a sinner. For years I had been blinded to the fact that I had sinned so much before this, but it was more hidden (and dare I say "acceptable") in Christian culture than anger and other outward sins.

But God, in His good grace, continues to show me what His grace is. Grace is His unmerited favor. And it's changed me. It continues to change me. It's changed my parenting and relationships. We all need grace! Without grace, our hearts/souls wither and dry up, and they become hardened.

How's your heart today, dear friend? Is it shriveled and dry? Or is it moist with fresh water, retaining it as healthy soil does? Hebrews 12:15 gives us a warning about a lack of grace in our hearts: "See to it that no one falls short of the grace of God and that no bitter root grows up to cause trouble and defile many."[7]

7. NIV.

We need grace in our relationships. Dallas Willard wisely said, "A carefully cultivated heart will, assisted by the grace of God, foresee, forestall, or transform most of the painful situations before which others stand like helpless children saying 'Why?'"[8]

AMENDMENT OF PULLING OUT THE WEEDS (REPENTANCE)

Weeds. They grow pretty much anywhere, don't they? You can even find weeds growing between the cracks in the sidewalk on a summer day. All they need is a little bit of soil and some water, and off they go! In our garden and orchard, if we don't keep on top of the weeds towards the end of spring, they can take over our crops and walking space. Two winters ago, SoCal received a record-breaking amount of rainfall. Where we live, we received 208 percent more rainfall than what is considered normal. Amongst friends and acquaintances, we have all shared our amazement and the dread of all of the happy weeds in our gardens and yards.

If left unattended, weeds steal precious nutrients from the soil, spread more seeds if not pulled up in time, and crowd the intentional produce and plants. We had to develop a habit of pulling weeds regularly in our garden. As you may remember in my opening story of getting serious about gardening, I started with pulling out so many overgrown weeds in the garden bed. The first thing I had to do was clear the soil of weeds before I could do anything else! This, my friend, is like the skill of repentance. Repentance is pulling pesky weeds out of the garden regularly.

The Greek New Testament word for "repent" is *metanoia*, which means "to change the mind."

To do a 180.

To do an about-face and forward march.

To completely change direction.

Specifically, it is to turn from sin and dedicate oneself to God. John the Baptist said to the Pharisees and Sadducees, "Produce

8. Willard, "Quotes about Heart."

fruit in keeping with repentance" (Matt 3:8).[9] A teacher and friend of ours, Steven Manuel, likes to call repentance "waving the white flag of surrender and saying, 'I need a Savior here!'"[10]

My eyes were opened to the habit and skill of repentance a couple of years ago while I was participating in my first *Story-Formed Life* experience (as referenced before). On the week we studied the skill of repentance, the facilitator sent us the link to a YouTube video named "Repentance Activation."[11] I have returned to this video many times to help me in times where I feel stuck in my walk with God and can't figure out why. There is a class that has transformed my walk with God more than anything else called Critical Skills and Strongholds, taught by our friend Steven Manuel. Highly recommended for every Christian. Just do it.

I believe repentance has often been misunderstood in our culture and generation. Many people believe, as did I, that repentance is something you do only once when you first turn to Jesus and believe in Him for your salvation. It's something you see on posters from street evangelists that say "repent or burn in hell." It's easy to form a misunderstanding about repentance even from these two examples. That's why we need some *solid* teaching on repentance.

In Luke 13:3,[12] Jesus says, "You will perish, too, unless you repent of your sins and turn to God." Repentance is an ongoing habit. We must understand this correctly and biblically.

What do we need to repent from?

Sin and dead works (Heb 6:1).

Ephesians 2:10 says that God has a specific list of things He created you to do. Dead works are works that aren't on God's list (including sin), such as doing things out of fear, shame, guilt, or pride. We can get in real trouble when we start to copy other people and what they're doing. (This sure highlights the problem of social media right now, doesn't it?) If you're not sure if something

9. NIV.
10. Critical Skills, "Critical Skills and Strongholds."
11. "Repentance Activation."
12. NLT.

that you're doing or praying about doing is a dead work, people in your community can help you call them out. And ask the Lord to show you. In 1 Cor 3:13, Paul is saying that our work "will be shown for what it is. It will be revealed with fire, and the fire will test the quality of each person's work."[13]

Jealousy and comparison can lead us into dead works. Legalism is a dead work; it's living under the law and putting your hope in your works-based righteousness.

We would do well to heed the many times in Scripture where this is cautioned against.

James tells us,

> Come near to God, and he will come near to you. Wash your hands, you sinners, and purify your hearts, you double-minded. Grieve, mourn and wail. Change your laughter to mourning and your joy to gloom. Humble yourselves before the Lord, and he will lift you up (Jas 4:8–10).[14]

There is something to be said about grieving our sin. I mean, really, *really* grieving it. That gut-wrenching, on-your-knees plea, "God, I'm sick of this, I repent and *need* You to fill me as I turn to You and repent of my sin towards You." I've had my share of those moments, for sure. I liken it to throwing up, honestly (sorry, gross, I know). You just can't keep going like that. Your body violently rejects whatever is in your stomach and gets rid of whatever is harming it—whether it be food poisoning, a virus, etc.

With repentance, it's not just a "God, I'm sorry for my sin. Help me to be a better person. Amen." No, God is not interested in sin management to abate our pride. It's like David in the Psalms: "God, I have sinned against you; please have mercy on me. Create in me a pure heart, O God, restore me to yourself. My sacrifice is a broken and contrite heart unto you" (my paraphrase of Ps 51). Do you see it? There's more to it than "I'm sorry."

---

13. NIV.
14. NIV.

Let's talk about sin for a second. Yeah, let's go there. Sin isn't just "doing bad stuff." The English word "sin" actually has its origins in an archery term that means "to miss the mark." There is a desired target, a law, that God gives us, but when we sin, we miss the target. We fall short. "The law of God is the target by which we measure where we fall short."[15] God has given us His laws in His love. I wish people truly understood that. His commandments are made out of love, because He knows what is best for us. When we sin, we're not trusting Him or believing that His way will lead to life.

Repentance is a change of heart, a deep sorrow for the sin done against a holy, good, great God. *This* is the heart posture that "produces fruit in keeping with repentance" (Matt 3:8).[16]

If this is resonating with you, I really encourage you to watch this "Repentance Activation" video or find a local Critical Skills and Strongholds class. It was profoundly eye-opening and transformative for me.

The opposite of repentance is a prideful, unforgiving heart. This is like the hard soil heart we've explored already. A prideful heart is deceived and unreceptive to grace, love, and forgiveness.

We need to also practice repentance in our earthly relationships. We must extend repentance to our spouse, children, boss, coworker, mother- or father-in-law, neighbors, etc. Again, not just "I'm sorry" (which doesn't cost much) but a genuine "I'm sorry, I was so wrong to do that, will you please forgive me?" type of repentance apology. Pull out those weeds, friend!

Dietrich Bonhoeffer said, "In a word, live together in the forgiveness of your sins, for without it no human fellowship, least of all a marriage, can survive."[17] No good fruit can grow in a garden overgrown and crowded with weeds of unforgiveness.

---

15. "Missing the Mark."
16. NIV.
17. Bonhoeffer, *Letters and Papers*, 31.

AMENDMENT OF NUTRIENTS (COMMUNITY)

Another amendment needed for healthy, fertile, good soil is nutrients. Without the appropriate and balanced amount of nutrients in the soil, it's just plain dirt, and a plant cannot grow in infertile dirt. In our lives, nutrients are like our community.

Community is where we are transformed.

We need many different types of people in our lives in order to thrive. Community is all about *inter*dependence (not independence). We know deep down that we need each other. No man or woman is an island. Community means we have a sense of responsibility for each other and rely on each other. We like the term "covenant community," where it's not your usual small group but rather an interdependent group of families and individuals who are dedicated to each other, on the good and bad days, seeking to live out Acts 2:42 biblically, together. People in our community are our spouses, parents, children, extended families, church families, neighbors, schoolmates, coworkers, and people at our local Trader Joe's or favorite coffee shops. These people in our lives fulfill different roles in our lives—family, mentors, neighbors, mentees. I've heard it said that it's optimal to aim to always have someone mentoring you who is years ahead of you and to be mentoring someone who is years younger than you. It's almost like the circle of life, "community style!"

Healthy soil interestingly parallels the facets of the community that we just covered. Living soil consists of a healthy balance of six essential nutrients: nitrogen, phosphorus, potassium, magnesium, sulfur, and calcium.[18]

Nitrogen and magnesium aid in strengthening the leaf development of the plants in the soil and are responsible for giving the leaves their green coloring by helping with chlorophyll production.[19] This is often how *mentors* are in our lives, whether they be parents, teachers, pastors, or simply someone further on in their

18. "6 Essential Nutrients."
19. "6 Essential Nutrients."

journey of life who speaks into ours. They add such richness and wisdom when we let them into our lives and take the time to listen. They can come alongside us in hard times and encourage us by sharing their stories of hope.

Phosphorus is responsible for helping with the root and flower growth. Interestingly, phosphorus also helps with strengthening plants so they can withstand environmental stress and harsh weather. This can represent the *people that are closest to us in our lives*. Our spouse (if applicable) or closest family or friends. These are the people that know you intimately and come alongside you in the great times and the challenging times of your life. They are not "fair-weather friends." They are committed people that speak life into you over the years.

Some dahlia blooms.

Potassium bolsters plants, contributes to early growth, and helps to retain water. Potassium also helps to act as an immune system to the plant.

The *New York Post* wrote in 2021 that "a recent survey found that the majority of Americans have fewer friends than they did three decades ago . . . and that Americans report having fewer close friendships than they once did, talking to their friends less often, and relying less on their friends for personal support."[20]

Part of this can be attributed to the fact that Americans are marrying later in life and traveling more, which both lead to a lack of depth in any friendships when that is the lifestyle people are after. A lack of rootedness in life can create a lack of deep friendships. It makes me think of this verse in Proverbs: "Let *love* and *faithfulness* [rootedness, adherence, fidelity, loyalty, dependability] never leave you; bind them around your neck, write them on the tablet of your heart. Then you will win favor and a good name in the sight of God and man" (Prov 3:3–4).[21]

Sulfur aids the plants in resisting disease and also helps the plant form seeds in the right timing. It also helps in the production of amino acids, proteins, enzymes, and vitamins.[22] This is like the *church family*—the family of God where we grow as disciples and equip and encourage others to make disciples, too (multiplying seeds). Dietrich Bonhoeffer said, "The Church is the Church only when it exists for others . . . not dominating, but helping and serving."[23] The role of the church family is irreplaceable in a Christian's life. It is essential. When we isolate ourselves from the church, we are susceptible to "disease," much like the lack of sulfur in soil—we are easier targets for the enemy to discourage us and cause doubt to spring up in our hearts. Just as a single wayward sheep is easy prey for a wolf, that's the reality for a Christian who strays from gathering with the family of God.

---

20 Cost, "Americans Have Fewer Friends."

21. NIV; added explanation mine.

22. "6 Essential Nutrients."

23. Bonhoeffer, *Letters and Papers*, 382–83.

The last nutrient that is essential to the health of soil is calcium. Calcium helps in the area of growth and the development of cell walls. This is very important because well-developed cell walls help the plant resist disease and help to keep a healthy metabolism for the plant to take in nitrogen.[24] This can represent *having healthy, biblical boundaries* in friendships and relationships. Please do not misunderstand me—I am not talking about "toxic people" and writing people off. Yes, we do need to know when to draw healthy boundaries with anyone in our lives who is causing hurt repeatedly. But Jesus didn't write people off or "cancel" people because they disagreed with Him, lashed out at Him, or spoke against Him. They weren't His close friends, that's for sure, but He didn't "cancel" them. Many Pharisees argued with Jesus and claimed wrong things about Him, and He continued to speak truth and teach about the Kingdom of God. He called out people for what they were doing but never out of meanness, nor did He shun them.

As Christians, we are commanded to not be "unequally yoked" with unbelievers. Do you know why? A yoke represents a uniting of heart, walking in the same direction in life, teaming up with someone. If you are in a close relationship with an unbeliever, which way do you think you'll end up going: the way of righteousness or wickedness?[25] First Corinthians 15:33[26] also tells us, "Bad company corrupts good character," or, as the Contemporary English Version says plainly, "Bad friends will destroy you."[27]

Boundaries can look different in relationships. We have to draw boundaries for ourselves in our lives. Peter Scazzero has a wonderful series of books through his organization called Emotionally Healthy Spirituality, and he talks a lot about embracing limits in our lives. "Limits" is not a word we hear a lot about in our culture today. We live in a day and age of "no limits." We see it in our culture in the ways of lifestyle choices and social media. Social media gives us the illusion of omnipotence and omnipresence (no

24. "6 Essential Nutrients."
25. See 2 Cor 6:14.
26. NIV.
27. CEV.

limits!). We hear messages such as "you can be anything you want if you work hard enough" or "you can do anything!" We know those ideas are lies but live like they are true. And it produces a ton of anxiety in our hearts.

That's why Adam and Eve sinned in the garden in Gen 3. God had given them the boundary (the *limit*) in saying that they could eat from any tree in the garden except for the tree of the knowledge of good and evil. God gave them a limit, but Adam and Eve wanted *more*. They weren't satisfied with what God had given them; therefore, they stepped out of their God-given limits and sinned against God and themselves.

We do the same today.

We overeat.

We overwork ourselves and forsake keeping a weekly sabbath.

We over-schedule our calendar.

We outspend our monthly budget.

We say "yes" to things that God never called us to.

And when we say "yes" to these things, we could actually be saying "no" to what God's original plan is. So, drawing boundaries in our lives is a healthy part of cultivating a resilient and whole heart, especially in our world today.

AMENDMENT OF HEALTHY ROOTS
(MEDITATING ON GOD'S TRUTH)

Once in the soil, the root of the plant is a vital part of its health. The root is the way the plant absorbs water and nutrients and stays anchored in the soil. Roots closely represent our thoughts. Whatever substance the roots (like our minds and hearts) are soaking up, the plant will reflect. If the plant is getting adequate water and nutrients, the fruit will show the effects of that. You've probably seen the elementary school experiment where you compare placing a celery stalk in a vase of clear water to another celery stalk in a vase of water with many drops of food coloring. After many hours, the stalk that is immersed in the food coloring will start to change color, then the leaves. This experiment illustrates the truth that what we allow to be in our "soil" affects the crop—the outcome of our lives.

Our hearts soak up whatever is around us: our environment, media, people/relationships, the habits we've formed, words people say to us. That's why the Bible gives us a very helpful list of what to fill our minds with when Paul told the Philippians in 4:8,

> Finally, brothers and sisters, whatever is true, whatever is noble, whatever is right, whatever is pure, whatever is lovely, whatever is admirable—if anything is excellent or praiseworthy—think about such things.[28]

This exhortation is preceded by a treasured passage of Scripture that Paul describes as a way to live our lives, and interestingly, what we just read in verse 8 is the how-to for verses 4–7:

> Rejoice in the Lord always. I will say it again: Rejoice! Let your gentleness be evident to all. The Lord is near. Do not be anxious about anything, but in every situation, by prayer and petition, with thanksgiving, present your requests to God. And the peace of God, which transcends all understanding, will guard your hearts and your minds in Christ Jesus (Phil 4:4–7).[29]

How do we rejoice in the Lord always? Whatever is true, whatever is noble . . .

How do we let our gentleness be evident to all? Whatever is right, whatever is pure . . .

How do we remind ourselves that the Lord is near? Whatever is lovely and admirable . . .

How do we not be anxious about anything? Whatever is excellent or praiseworthy . . .

Do you see it now? Our thoughts are extremely important.

This relates to a verse we studied earlier, Prov 4:23: "Above all else, guard your heart [your thoughts], for everything you do flows from it."[30]

28. NIV.
29. NIV.
30. NIV; words added are mine.

I went through a time in my motherhood where I was stuck in negativity. It was a really difficult season. I woke up to the "daily grind" every morning, had my quiet time with God, made my decaf coffee (sad, I know, but I needed to step away from caffeine for a bit), and got ready to meet our five children to start the day. Our family homeschools, so I am with them most of the day. The constant sound and motion can be a blessed challenge for this high-functioning introverted mama on some days.

But I discovered that I had gotten stuck in a negative way of thinking—and it came out in my words and eventually made me depressed. I admit I had some days where I felt a victim of our choice to homeschool, as hard as that was for me to admit that. I've gone through seasons where I was not "taking captive every thought to make it obedient to Christ" (2 Cor 10:5).[31] Friend, if you do not put boundaries on your thoughts, you will be at the mercy of your thoughts. We *must* take every thought captive and make it obedient to Christ and choose to dwell on whatever is true, right, etc. (Phil 4:8).

I feel this to be true more now than any other time in history, when there is a war on truth. I'm speaking from experience that you will be a sunken ship if you neglect to keep your thoughts in check. The world and the enemy are ready and willing to fill your thoughts with ideas, lies, and distractions that pull you away from God. This is an area we must be resolute about. Again, I'm unfortunately speaking from experience . . .

One of my favorite quotes about our thoughts is from a missionary and heroine of the faith, Elisabeth Elliot. She knew a thing or two about thoughts and suffering and living for God.

She said,

> Refuse self-pity. *Refuse it absolutely.* It is a deadly thing with the power to destroy you. Turn your thoughts to Christ who has already carried your griefs and sorrows.[32]

Did you catch that phrase?

31. NIV.
32. Wickey, "Writers' Corner"; emphasis mine.

47

It is a deadly thing with the power to destroy you.

Well said, Elisabeth Elliot. She knew what she was talking about. She was the wife of a murdered missionary, and she turned around and shared the gospel with the very people who killed her husband. And they believed. That is so honorable, and I can bet you she was able to do that only in the Holy Spirit's power and by taking her thoughts captive and not falling into self-pity. Oh, how sad to think if she had chosen the opposite. What if she had wallowed in self-pity after her husband died? She wouldn't have turned around and ministered to the Auca tribe; she would have fled back to comfort in America, I can bet!

I had a moment recently where two dots were connected for me. My friends in my community were gathering for a women's group, and we began talking about Psalm 1. After discussing the psalm and what stood out to us, we all decided that we loved the part "...but whose delight is in the law of the LORD, and who meditates on his law day and night" (Ps 1:2).[33]

I had a moment of connection as I looked behind me in our backyard where my husband had laid many yards of irrigation line in our new garden beds. We had tomatoes and peppers on one side that were growing like mad, and they were so lush and a vibrant green color. My husband had shared with me that he programmed the irrigation to water the garden beds twice a day—once in the early morning and again in the evening. Interesting. And God showed me that this is what He was talking about in Ps 1. We need regular watering from the Word of God day and night into our hearts. "May these words of my mouth and this meditation of my heart be pleasing in Your sight, O Lord, my Rock and my Redeemer" (Ps 19:14).[34]

I end this "amendment" with a quote from Dallas Willard:

> The ultimate freedom we have as human beings is the power to select what we will allow our minds to dwell upon. It is in our thoughts that the first movements

33. NIV.
34. NIV.

toward the renovation of the heart occur. Thoughts are the place where we can and must begin to change.[35]

AMENDMENT OF SUNLIGHT
(GOD'S PRESENCE AND PRAYER)

I grew up in Oregon near Portland (before it was cool). We Oregonians get a bad rap for enduring large amounts of rainfall every year. Growing up, I honestly didn't know any different, and we just played outside if it was raining without a second thought. We intuitively knew that when the sun peaked its introverted head out in the spring, you dropped everything you were doing indoors and you got yourself outside. ASAP. In high school, shorts were worn immediately when the weather turned sixty degrees. Sunlight was a *big deal* for three quarters of the year.

I remember hearing a family friend of ours tell us about a time when he announced to his family one day in the middle of a dreary spring day, "OK, kids, I'm hopping in the van, and I'm driving south on I-5 until I see the sun! Who's coming with me?" Sunlight deprivation is a real thing, y'all.

Sunlight is needed for survival. Concerning our bodies, many studies have proven that sunlight is vital to our wellbeing. Studies have shown that sunlight can reduce high blood pressure, regulate the immune system, strengthen bones, improve sleep quality, and boost moods. If a person does not get adequate sunlight exposure, there are many health problems that can arise.

Sunlight exposure aids in the production of the hormones serotonin and melatonin. If you mess with your levels, you mess with your circadian rhythm. Sunlight also produces vitamin D in our bodies. Studies have been showing that cases of cancer rise in people with low levels of vitamin D. It's so unfortunate that "Americans spend ninety percent of their time indoors on average."[36] Interestingly, a person can live without sunlight, albeit

35. Willard, *Renovation of the Heart*, 95.
36. "Light Deprivation."

it is not recommended. So, it's possible to live your life without direct sunlight on your body, but it would be detrimental to your health, both short-term and long-term and in all areas of your wellbeing—physical, emotional, relational, and spiritual.

Concerning the physical earth, it cannot survive without sunlight. Here's an interesting take on what would happen if the sun disappeared:

> Light takes roughly eight minutes to reach Earth from the sun. For that reason, if the sun disappeared, we'd still see it in the sky for another eight minutes. But what about gravity? The sun is the anchor point of the solar system—at 333,000 times the mass of Earth, it exerts a hefty pull that keeps the planets locked in their orbits. If all that gravitational force disappeared, it would still take us eight minutes to feel it. That's because, according to Einstein's theory of relativity, gravity travels at the same speed as light. So go ahead, watch the rest of that Netflix episode. You'll be golden for another eight minutes.
>
> After that, though, Earth still wouldn't be snuffed out. Electricity would still work, and it would still take up to an hour for the light from our planets to be reflected back to Earth, so there would be a peaceful glow in the sky. With no sunlight, photosynthesis would stop, but that would only kill some of the plants—there are some larger trees that can survive for decades without it. Within a few days, however, the temperatures would begin to drop, and any humans left on the planet's surface would die soon after. Within two months, the ocean's surface would freeze over, but it would take another thousand years for our seas to freeze solid. By then, however, the atmosphere would collapse, radiation would seep in, and Earth would be an inhospitable wasteland drifting aimlessly through space. Lucky for you, the sun is showing no signs of disappearing any time soon.[37]

We can see how sunlight is crucial to our survival. We cannot exist very long without it. It's our lifeline, and many things we need stem from the sun's existence. Sunlight travels through and

37. Hamer, "What Would Happen."

permeates the air all around us and fills it with light and warmth and life. It starts externally, then it gets into our bodies and creates health all over.

God's presence is like that.

What exactly *is* God's presence? Glad you asked.

First, a personal attempt, then one from the Bible.

You know that first moment of warm, bright sunlight after a week of cold winter weather? Couple that with a loving, warm hug from a loved one, along with a first bite of a warm, gooey chocolate chip cookie straight from the oven, and then a sharp rumbling of thunder in the near background. Combine all of those ingredients and multiply them by one thousand and you'll get a taste of what God's presence is like.

The Hebrew word for God's holy and favorable presence is *panim*, and it often refers to the face of God.[38] How beautiful, right? The presence of God is explained as His face toward us, towards you. The word *panim* occurs 2,100 times throughout the Bible, which is astounding and really says something.

Scripture is filled with many verses in which people are asking for God to shine upon them or turn His face towards them. Psalm 119:135[39] says, "Make Your face [*paneka*] shine upon Your servant, and teach me Your statutes."[40] The face of God illuminated everything, which was why so many biblical authors asked God to shine His face upon them. We see this in the garden where Adam and Eve initially walked with God (face to face), but when they chose to rebel against God, sin separated them from God and they were banished from the garden (from God's presence). That's why God sent His Son, Jesus, to pay the penalty for our rebellion so that we could be reconciled to God and see Him face to face again. The moment Jesus died, the temple curtain (which was about sixty feet high, sixty feet wide, and four inches thick!) was torn from top to bottom. We can now approach His presence without a barrier! Hallelujah! Thank you, Jesus!

38. "Reading Before the Face of God."

39. NIV.

40. "Panim/Paneh."

In the Old Testament, God's manifest presence went with the Israelites as He guided them out of Egypt and to the promised land. He came as the flames in a bush that appeared to be burning but never consumed, in a pillar of cloud by day, and a pillar of fire by night. In the New Testament and today, God's presence is now not only external—it's now inside each disciple because the Holy Spirit lives in us as His followers.

We must, as His disciples, spend time in His presence, as we must bask in the sunshine. I love how the biblical authors equated God's shining on them as the sun shines on us. It's crucial. It's our lifeline. Hearts need to be prepared before they can receive the Word and be saved and blessed. One main way for us to stay connected with God in His presence is through prayer. Prayer is simply talking to and listening to God. It's part of a real relationship. Brother Lawrence has his famous book that he called *The Practice of the Presence of God*. Whatever he was doing, he sought to be in communion with God. Staying in His presence. Abiding through prayer. "Don't seek to develop a prayer life—seek a praying life. A 'prayer life' is a segmented time for prayer . . . A 'praying life' is a life that is saturated with prayerfulness—you seek to do all that you do with the Lord."[41]

Jesus beautifully said in John 15:5:

> I am the vine, you are the branches. When you're joined with Me and I with you, the relation intimate and organic, the harvest is sure to be abundant.[42]

Dallas Willard said,

> You must arrange your days so that you are experiencing deep contentment, joy and confidence in your everyday life with God.[43]

If we don't stay connected to Him and choose to detach or disobey, Scripture has told us what can happen. In the middle of a

41. Gaultiere, "Dallas Willard's Definitions."

42. MSG.

43. As quoted in Olive, "Arranging Our Days."

long, encouraging list that Paul is writing to the Thessalonians, he adds, "Do not quench the Spirit" (1 Thess 5:19).[44]

In the Message paraphrase, it says, "Don't suppress the Spirit." Just as we pour water on a campfire before retiring to our tents on a camping trip, we can do that to the Spirit's work in our lives if we aren't obeying and attending to our hearts. To quench means to dampen, douse, or snuff out. Definitely not life-giving words. For example, when we are prompted to give that friend a call because we feel the Spirit nudging us to check in with them and pray with them, but we choose not to, we quench the Spirit's work in our lives.

I will share that there are times God's face seems hidden, and it's hard to discern why. Maybe you've experienced this too, dear friend? As we follow Jesus, there will be times in our lives where God feels distant for no obvious reason.

The season is often known as "the dark night of the soul." It encapsulates the times where it feels that we've been planted deep in dark soil without any sense or feeling of sunlight. I've experienced a couple of seasons like that, and they're so, so hard. But, if we "stay planted" (pardon the Christianese jargon) and trust God is still there and is at work, and we don't uproot what God is doing, we will poke our heads out of the dark dirt into the hope of a fruitful harvest and new deep-rootedness.

Before we put an end cap to this chapter, I've got to say a word about artificial sunlight. My amazing gardener husband educated me about it, as we have used it in our shed to start seedlings before planting them in the garden bed outside in the elements. Artificial sunlight is a wonderful invention to get those seeds sprouted and seedlings growing, but there's a limit to its effectiveness. Yes, you could actually grow a plant from seed to full-grown plant, *but* the health of the plant will be compromised at some point. Because it's *artificial* energy. It's not going to get you all the way to the goal.

Artificial sunlight eventually stunts the growth of the plants because it indirectly affects it by its environment. If a plant is under artificial sunlight, it's not outside in a garden bed. It's inside

44. NIV.

a shelter, away from direct sunlight, pests, wind, harsh temperatures, rain, and snow. We learned the hard way last year, when we transplanted seedlings *way* too late in the spring, that those seedlings must be exposed to the elements at a crucial point of their growth early on or they will be forever stunted and likely die when exposed to the elements.

It makes me think of the ways we often try to make it through our day—powered by something else than the Holy Spirit. Instead of staying connected to God in prayer and seeking His face, we settle for that third cup of coffee, or TV show to numb out a bit after a long day, or mindless scrolling through social media, or going shopping even though we don't really need anything. Artificial strength from something other than God will not last. These things aren't always bad in and of themselves, but if we *rely* on them for strength or to get us through our day, chances are that it's an idol and will eventually distance us from God and wreak havoc on our spiritual lives (for deeper study, check out Jeremiah 2).

AMENDMENT OF MARGIN
(ROOM TO GROW)

A plant cannot grow while crowded with weeds or other plants that are competing for its space. Just like the plants growing in soil, our hearts need margin. Room to grow. Wide open spaces. Interestingly, the Merriam-Webster definition of margin is "the part of a page or sheet outside the main body of printed or written matter; the outside limit and adjoining surface of something; edge."[45]

Another fitting definition and explanation I found is from the book *Margin: Restoring Emotional, Physical, Financial and Time Reserves to Overloaded Lives*:

> Margin is the space between our load and our limits. . .
> Margin is the gap between rest and exhaustion, the space
> between breathing freely and suffocating. Margin is the
> opposite of overload. If we are overloaded we have no

45. "Margin."

margin. Most people are not quite sure when they pass from margin to overload . . . We don't want to be underachievers (heaven forbid!), so we fill our schedules uncritically. Options are as attractive as they are numerous, and we overbook . . . Many people commit to a 120 percent life and wonder why the burden feels too heavy. It is rare to see a life prescheduled to only 80 percent, leaving a margin for responding to the unexpected that God sends our way.[46]

At the time of writing this chapter, my family and I are currently staying at an Airbnb in the middle of nowhere in northeastern Oregon. In all directions, we are surrounded by grain fields. It's August, so the fields are ripe for harvest and it's absolutely breathtaking. This SoCal-dwelling but Oregon-born mama is always craving wide open spaces. And boy, have we had that. It's been amazing to see our kids thrive in this environment. My husband and I have felt it, and we feel like our souls are taking a big, long exhale in these wide open spaces.

All living things need space to grow and thrive. Our gardens and hearts both need it. Constant activity, busyness, distraction, and demands easily crowd our days from staying connected to the True Vine (Jesus) that gives and sustains life.

Have you ever seen a crowded garden? I'll admit that there have been times where I've been sloppy in planting seeds. (Yes, it's true. . .) It is a general rule of thumb when directly sowing seeds that you should plant two seeds per space. This practice increases your chance of having at least one seedling sprout. Then, a week or so later, after both seeds have sprouted, you come and thin out the seedlings. You do this by pulling one of the two sprouted seeds in order for one to thrive and survive. It is always painful to pull up a new seedling, but if you don't, you compromise the health and fruitfulness of *both* plants!

I have had moments where I've not thinned out my plants because I want all of the seeds to stay in the ground and maybe have twice as many plants! That's short-term-Michelle's way of

---

46. Swenson, *Margin*, 69–70.

thinking. Future Michelle will thank present Michelle for wise decisions made now. Lack of space and margin will greatly affect the health of the plants.

Each plant needs its own space to thrive. It needs adequate space so it can get plenty of sunshine, nutrients from the soil, and water. On the back of seed packets you will always find a recommended spacing for planting the seeds in the soil. You'll see carrots spaced at two to three inches between plants. Beets spaced at two to four inches. Potatoes at three feet apart. Spinach at two inches. You get the picture. These plants need boundaries in order to survive. They need space to call their own which is not be encroached upon. Not to be selfish and hog all of the free resources but to remain healthy.

Our hearts are exactly the same. We must not overcrowd our hearts. This, my friends, is the task of our day. Our world is bent on a worldview of no limits: you can do anything you want, be anything you want, buy as much as you want (charge it!), have sex with whomever you want, write off whoever you want, label whoever you want, believe whatever you want. And do you know what the result of all of these limitless ideas is?

Anxiety.

Is anxiety a sign of life and freedom and peace?

Nope.

It's quite the opposite.

A principle of the universe is that worldly freedom brings slavery. We think that having the choice to do whatever we want is true freedom. But uninhibited freedom is not actually freedom—it's slavery. It enslaves us to our sinful nature. That freedom is not real freedom; it's a counterfeit. So, when we buy the world's belief that limitlessness is freedom, we believe and live a lie, and that wreaks havoc in our lives.

We must learn how to order our lives in a way that has margin. Thankfully, Jesus modeled this for us when He would frequently withdraw to pray. Luke 5:16 says, "Jesus often withdrew to lonely places and prayed."[47] This margin alone with His Father gave Him

47. NIV.

the strength to be with His disciples and crowds all day long, meeting their needs and teaching (sounds a lot like parenting!). Parents and caretakers, we especially have to be so proactive in this area to take care that we do not burn out!

Friends, in short, take care of your heart. Protect it. Watch over it.

What's this all for, anyway? (In conclusion to the amendments)

The reason for desiring good, living soil is for the purpose of a healthy crop. God desires for us to live life to the full (John 10:10) because we are rooted in Him, abide in Him, and draw our very life and meaning from Him. A passage that illustrates this is Phil 1:9–11 when Paul is encouraging the Philippians:

> And this is my prayer: that your love may abound more and more in knowledge and depth of insight, so that you may be able to discern what is best and may be pure and blameless for the day of Christ, filled with the fruit of righteousness that comes through Jesus Christ—to the glory and praise of God.[48]

48. NIV.

5

Dangers to Your Heart (and Garden)

JUST AS THERE ARE many amendments to contribute to soil and heart health, there are many things that can be dangerous to the soil and to our hearts. Again, we will take a close look at some shocking parallels.

DANGER OF HIGH SALINITY (COMPETING VOICES/DISTRACTIONS)

Soil and water naturally contain some salt. Too high salinity damages the soil. This means that the amount of salt in the water coming in outpaces the salt that is draining.[1] In this illustration, I imagine salt being the differing voices we hear during the day. Today, in 2025, most of those voices come from media sources: news, social media, email, mail, billboards, and various other forms of technology. Not all of these things are bad in and of themselves. But if we are not carefully discerning in this time in history, our hearts can become polluted by too much information and entertainment,

---

1. "Water Salinization."

which results in distraction—a lot like how too much salt acts in soil.

Andrew Sullivan from *New York Magazine* wrote a sobering and stunning article in 2016 entitled "I Used to Be a Human Being" in which the author coined the phrase "distraction sickness." His subtitle reads "An Endless Bombardment of News and Gossip and Images Has Rendered Us Manic Information Addicts. It Broke Me. It Might Break You, Too."[2]

mic drop

Can anyone else relate? Now, I've been privileged to read some amazing books around this subject that teach how to be disciplined with technology. And part of this book is my process of working through those resources. Synthesizing it, making it my own, and sharing it with others. Wading through the waters and coming out on the other side. I—like most people, I'd bet—have become addicted to my phone. As much as I wouldn't willingly lump myself into the "addict" or "compulsive checker" category, I've fallen into it from time to time. It usually happens in busy times (which is ironic) when I haven't had the space to slow down and think of what I'm actually doing. It's become an epidemic to check our phones in our first waking moments because our alarm goes off on our phone and we're already holding it.

Too much salt.

Too many voices competing for our attention.

Deadly to our soils and to our hearts.

Distractedness is killing our souls and hearts. Slowly. Under the radar. Much like the slow way salinity accumulates in soil. With every choice to turn to these devices, we are allowing more voices, more information to permeate our hearts. If we're constantly turning to these notifications and dings and scrolling mindlessly, our hearts get filled with unnecessary and cluttering images, words, and inside looks into strangers' lives who carry the weight of influence to our lives. If this salt accumulation is left unchecked, it *will* build to an unhealthy level.

2. Sullivan, "I Used to Be."

Toxicity.

Stress.

Discontentment.

Restlessness.

Inability to embrace quiet and be present.

Irritability.

Compulsive behaviors.

Each day more salt could be added to our hearts. A dash of salt here, a dash there. A little bit of Instagram, a little bit of You-Tube. A little bit of Pinterest, a little bit of news. Interestingly, a little bit of salt is very healthy and helps soil thrive. But too much is toxic and creates an environment opposite of thriving—actually, deterioration. Decline. Retrogress. A toxic environment. Salt can actually change the pH of the soil so that it blocks the nutrients available to the plants. Too much of an initially good thing acts counterproductively!

The only remedies to help soil become less salty is less salt intake or good drainage. And you may remember, water is grace to our hearts. If we have to engage with a lot of information because of work, or if your personality can easily process a lot of information, there is God's grace over that. But not all of us are wired like that. His grace compels us to stop scrolling because we know we don't have to prove our worth or value. We can disengage because we are secure in His love and our identity in Him. When we allow His voice to be the main voice and the voice we listen to above all others, our heart stays healthy. We must pay close attention to what we hear and the voices that compete for our attention. We live in an attention economy, where our attention is the commodity. Salt should be added and used, but it either gets absorbed into the growing plants for their thriving or it passes through as drainage.

We love to know the latest news and to be connected to people. That's why the printing press was invented, and Morse code, and many other means of communication. We yearn to be connected to people. But this has taken a dire turn the past twenty years. Mailed letters turned into email, which morphed with dial phones to create a flip phone, which evolved into the Blackberry, which gave way to the smartphone. And here we are. Almost limitless information at our fingertips, at breakneck speed.

All of this limitless information and freedom of access creates anxiety in our souls. We weren't created to imbibe this much information on a regular basis. All of this information makes us feel omnipresent and omniscient, which are characteristics that only God possesses. Of course the by-product of chasing after these two things brings anxiety. It's not intended for us! Let God be God, and let us be us, and make peace with that. Taking in so much information will easily make us hurried. John Mark Comer said, "Hurry is a form of violence on the soul."[3] We must put a boundary on how much salt we take in our soil.

DANGER OF ACIDIFICATION (COMPARISON)

Pinterest. A social media idea that acted as gasoline dumped on the insecurity and struggle we all have with comparison today. At least in my experience.

> Traditionally, Pinterest has seen more use among women than men. The report indicates that Pinterest reaches 60 percent of all US women, including 80 percent of moms and 75 percent of millennial women.[4]

Whoa.

I had a very distinct moment with Pinterest in 2012. Since it was made available to the public in 2010, Pinterest has been a hotspot of resources, greed, comparison, and coveting. I had heard of it in 2012, and I was curious. I vividly remember the first moment I went on the Pinterest website. I found my friend's page who had raved about it and immediately I felt this heavy spirit of covetousness on it, and it actually made me sick to my stomach. But there was this other side of me that was curious and wanted to stockpile photos, recipes, and kids' craft ideas for myself so I wasn't

3. Comer, *Ruthless Elimination*, 47.
4. Southern, "Pinterest."

missing out. After all, it *was* handy to have all of those websites and resources right at my fingertips! I remember sitting still at our computer, weighing it in my mind.

I chose to start a profile. And, to be fair, Pinterest has been a helpful tool at times, but sadly, I know it played a big role in my formation for a couple of years. I became the mom who poured herself a cup of coffee at nap time and headed to my computer for an hour—on Pinterest. Ugh. I mourn the hours I wasted, honestly. Sure, it was fun to have an inspiration for creative outlets and share pins with friends and such, but it formed me in ways that I'm still unlearning today. These became my inward thoughts:

My house has to look like hers, or I'm failing as a homemaker.

My kids need to do this craft, or I'm failing as a mother.

I need to have that outfit because I feel discontent with the clothes that I have.

I need to pin that recipe so I can make stellar dinners for my family. (Ever seen Pinterest Fails? Yes, friends, it's a thing—I should have posted a couple myself!)

My workout schedule and house cleaning schedule stinks—I should be doing more.

Oh, look at that devotional that mom did with her kids—I should do that, too.

Some other thoughts we may struggle with are:

I'm not enough.

I'm too much.

If I mean well, that's good enough.

And on and on it can go, my friends. I'm still bringing some of these lies to God for healing and exchanging them for His truth. If we're not careful, comparison can eat us alive. It's the same with the soil in a garden. Acidic soils are referred to as "sour." Slightly acidic soil is healthy, but if a soil is too acidic, it can cause plant poisoning. There are a couple of plants, such as potatoes, blueberries, and many deciduous trees, that prefer acidic soil. But generally, the rest of the plants in the world prefer soil that is not too acidic.

Our hearts are like that. Envy and jealousy—or our more widely accepted label "comparison"—sour our hearts quickly like acidity in soil. Theodore Roosevelt wisely said, "Comparison is the thief of joy,"[5] and his niece, Eleanor Roosevelt, interestingly said, "No one can make you feel inferior without your consent."[6]

Of course Scripture has something to say about that. Second Corinthians 10:12[7] says,

> Not that we dare to classify or compare ourselves with some of those who are commending themselves. But when they measure themselves by one another and compare themselves with one another, they are without *understanding.*

There's that word again—*understanding.*

A phrase that I repeat to my children often is, "You cannot control others; you can only control yourself." We have enough work to be concerned about with ourselves! When we try to overstep in someone else's life, ugh, that's no good, and it's too much for us!

The Rabbi Zusya is quoted with saying, "In the coming world, they will not ask me: 'Why were you not Moses?' They will ask me: 'Why were you not Zusya?'"[8] We are to focus on God to make us into the person He created us to be, and not comparing ourselves to others.

Scripture tells us,

> Do *your* best to present *yourself* to God as one approved, a worker who has no need to be ashamed, rightly handling the word of truth (2 Tim 2:15).[9]

Also, I love what the great philosopher and psychologist Jordan Peterson says: "Compare yourself to who you were yesterday, not to who someone else is today."[10] But we have to be careful of this, as it could turn into an ego trip if not kept in check.

5 Quoted in Steiner, "Comparison."

6. Roosevelt and Clarke, "No One."

7. ESV; emphasis mine.

8. Scazzero, "Peter Scazzero Quotes."

9. ESV; emphasis mine.

10. Peterson, *12 Rules for Life*, 85.

DANGER OF POLLUTION
(MATERIALISM)

We live in a time of many, many resources, here in the West in particular. We have so many material resources, technological resources, educational resources. We have more options than is healthy for our souls. An easy example of this is going to the grocery store for a jar of applesauce. Instead of finding the aisle and grabbing the jar of applesauce, you must arrive at the aisle and be met with a wide array of applesauces. You can spend minutes deciding between different brands, different sizes, different flavors. Too many choices bring anxiety—studies have proven it.[11] Professor Renata Salecl called it and named her book *The Tyranny of Choice*. Too many choices are just plain harsh on our souls.

There's actually a phrase to describe this experience: "choice overload" (also known as "overchoice," "choice paralysis," or "the paradox of choice").[12] Boy, have I been there. That's why I love simple restaurant menus or coffee shops that focus on a handful of items to choose from—it simplifies life for me! We think having more options gives us more freedom to choose what we want, but it actually welcomes anxiety.

In our society, it is not hard to find a person with a cluttered mind, a cluttered house, and a cluttered schedule. These three areas of life must be guarded and stewarded well.

Having too many things around us creates clutter—our hearts can't breathe. Just as weeds, grasses, yard stuff, and trash can clutter up a garden, so our hearts are cluttered up by a surplus of different types of things. These things can be physical clutter (too many things in a room), emotional clutter (carrying unresolved emotions), and intellectual clutter (too many things on our minds, or "too many tabs open" as I like to call it—my favorite expression of this reality).

In Jan Johnson's wonderful book *The Abundance of Simplicity*, she says,

11. Jeffries, "Why Too Much Choice."
12. "Why Do We Have."

The point of simplicity is not efficiency, increased productivity or even living a healthier, more relaxed life. The
point is making space for treasuring God's own self. [13]

In our experience in owning and tending to a garden, we've
seen the importance of keeping on top of the clutter. We have to
make sure to throw away any trash that can land on the soil—bags
from Home Depot, old cracked plant pots, and discarded supplies
such as string and stakes. Pollution in the air can also affect soil.
"Air pollutants that are first deposited on the soil, such as heavy
metals, first affect the functioning of roots and interfere with soil
resource capture by the plant."[14]

Visual clutter is like materialism in our souls. The spiritual
discipline of simplicity has gained a lot of popularity through modern minimalism. There is so much good that has come from this
movement, but it is easy for it to turn into an idol in and of itself.
We must be careful and discerning. Minimalism is a means to an
end, not an end in itself. But if we are curating our surroundings in
order to help us make space for God, we can't go wrong! When we
hang on to too much stuff (physical and emotional), only negative
things come from it. Perhaps you've seen the TV show *Hoarders*?
It's interesting . . . and very sad. It's a show centered around people
who have held onto so much stuff, and it's stealing their quality of
life. You can see how people's hearts are entangled with their things
on this earth.

Studies have been done about the connection between visual
clutter and stress levels. Put simply, never before has a generation
had to deal with a surplus of materials and learn how to manage it.[15]

more stuff = more stress

As a homeschooling mom of five children ages fifteen and
under, stuff is a major thing to manage in our household. The past
three years in late spring, my husband and I have decided to rent
a dumpster and fill it with unwanted, unnecessary items. We also

13. Johnson, *Abundant Simplicity*, 10.
14. Weber and Andersen, "Plant Response."
15. Fuller, "How Clutter and Mental Health."

make multiple trips to our local Goodwill. After a week of purging, we feel lighter! It has forced us to be choosy about the things we *do* treasure and helps us live out our values as a family.

We must watch over our schedules, also. I've heard pastors say, "If you want to find out what are the most important things in a person's life, look at their calendar and their checkbook." Whew! What is important to us makes it onto our calendars, and is also what we spend our money on.

DANGER OF COMFORT AND COMPLACENCY (WATERLOGGING)

Is there such a thing as too much of a good thing? Yes, actually, in gardening. It's called waterlogging. Waterlogging happens when soil gets so saturated with water that it reduces the oxygen available to the roots. This causes yellowing of the leaves, rotting of the roots, and eventually death. I've found this to happen especially in my potted plants if there is not sufficient drainage. If there are not any drainage holes at the bottom of the pot, the water poured on the soil seeps to the bottom and just rots. It's not a pretty sight, nor delightful to the nose, either. Putrid soil smells so nasty.

When water does not have a conduit, or a way to channel water to another place, it becomes putrid and smelly. Think of an old pond that is slowly evaporating in the summer after it was filled by the spring rains, filled with green algae and brown murky water. I recently heard an interview where pastor Darren Rouanzoin from Garden Church in Huntington Beach, California, said, "Comfort leads to compromise."[16]

Waterlogging is a lot like when we cease to be a conduit of God's grace. We have no trouble receiving God's grace, but then we decide that it stops with us. We're *comfortable* being on the receiving end of grace, but somehow there's not been a heart change where giving grace is happening. This can often happen because of unforgiveness that is being harbored in the heart. Or selfishness,

16. Pastorate, "Incubator Sessions."

or envy. These are things that we need to be watching over in the garden of our hearts. Jesus teaches us, "For if you forgive other people when they sin against you, your heavenly Father will also forgive you. But if you do not forgive others their sins, your Father will not forgive your sins." (Matt 6:14–15).[17]

The interesting parallel here is that smelly soil is like a smelly heart. A decaying patch of soil is like a person with a graceless heart, where you wince when you're in the presence of them. There have been times where I've been led to remember the words of Paul in Heb 12:15:[18] "See to it that no one falls short of the grace of God and that no bitter root grows up to cause trouble and defile many."

Here is the same passage from The Message:

> Make sure no one gets left out of God's generosity. Keep a sharp eye out for weeds of bitter discontent. A thistle or two gone to seed can ruin a whole garden in no time.

Do you see that? In this paraphrase, gardening is used to illustrate this truth! (Thank you, Eugene Peterson . . .)

If we are constantly listening to sermons and worship music and reading books, but there is no conduit for living out what is being learned, our souls can turn rancid and stale. When we hear and/or read the Word of God, we are to obey and *act* on it in faith! No passive listening allowed! The litmus test for our love for God is found in 1 John 2:3: "And by this we know that we have come to know Him, if we keep His commandments."[19]

We experience this daily as a family. We are intentional parents, but boy, we're far from having it all figured out. We gather every weekday morning as a family at home to study the Word together. Often we approach it with the Discovery Bible Study (DBS) method, and sometimes our kids take turns facilitating it with our guidance. At the end of a DBS, a question is asked to the group, "How can I apply this in my life this week?," with the expectation

17. NIV.
18. NIV.
19. ESV.

that we will all do what we said. For about six months, we noticed that we weren't following up on this question, and it didn't sit well with us. We were unintentionally being hearers of the Word only and not doers in this situation. Not OK. So now we are aiming to check in with each other intentionally, writing it on our chalkboard wall in the hallway so it's close to our minds and hearts.

James exhorts us, "Do not merely listen to the word, and so deceive yourselves. *Do what is says.* Anyone who listens to the word but does not do what it says is like someone who looks at his face in a mirror and, after looking at himself, goes away and immediately forgets what he looks like" (Jas 1:22–24[20]).

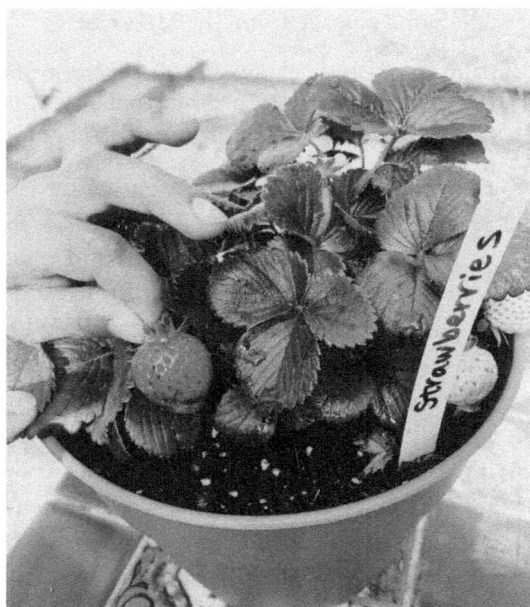

Soil with good drainage produces healthy crops.

God has created this life for us to not just consume but to be a conduit of His grace and truth. When we are doers of the Word, this takes place. Be a conduit, not a stale, stinky pond.

20. NIV; emphasis mine.

DANGER OF SOIL COMPACTION

(Unforgiveness and Hardness of Heart)

I touched a bunch on this topic in previous chapters. But to reiterate (as we all need it!), hard soil is like a hard and neglected heart. Perhaps the soil is hardened from others trampling on it. Perhaps it is hard because of walls put up to protect from further hurt or misunderstandings. Perhaps it's plain rebellion. Regardless of the reason for the callous soil/heart, the reality is that it is hard.

And unyielding.

And unfruitful.

And "hardheaded."

But . . .

not impossible to make soft again.

Through God's grace (water) and some good ol' tilling, you are to "break up your fallow ground" (Hos 10:12 and Jer 4:3). There are a couple of times in Scripture that God tells us to do this. To break up fallow ground means to till up earth that has been lying fallow (dormant/unused) so that it may become more fruitful and cleared of thorns and weeds. One way to interpret this is, "So says the prophet, 'Break off your evil ways, repent of your sins, cease to do evil, and then the good seed of the word will have room to grow and bear fruit.'"[21]

> This is what the LORD says to the people of Judah and to Jerusalem: "Sow righteousness for yourselves, reap the fruit of unfailing love, and break up your unplowed ground; for it is time to seek the LORD, until he comes and showers his righteousness on you"(Hos 10:12[22]).

> Break up your unplowed ground and do not sow among thorns (Jer 4:3[23]).

A last illustration about hard soil: carrots must be planted in soil that is really light, airy, and tilled thoroughly, or the carrots

21. "Fallow-ground."

22. NIV.

23. NIV.

grow all crooked and stunted. Anytime you see long, beautiful carrots means that the farmer understands this principle. I've seen (and grown) a fair share of crooked and stunted carrots. We must till up the ground so that it is not hard but rather soft, airy, and receptive. We must confess, become open, and surrender our hearts to God.

DANGER OF PESTS
(THE WORLD, THE FLESH, THE DEVIL)

June is a time of the year that many gardeners detest, as far as bugs go. Once a year in June, the Japanese beetle emerges and wreaks havoc on gardens and people alike. These half-inch-long bugs fly clumsily through the air, buzzing loudly and landing in unwanted places. I have a friend who has beautiful, voluminous black hair, and while exiting church one day, one of these bugs flew straight into her hair and started to nest in it. I was scarred for life to witness it, as well as she was.

These green, metallic, and shiny bugs aren't just an aerial nuisance. The biggest nuisance is in the ground and around crops. "The *Old Farmer's Almanac* names Japanese beetles as one of the most troublesome pests of the eastern and midwestern parts of the country."[24] These pests start as grubs in the soil and will feed unseen on the roots of plants in a garden, grow to emerge as adults, and feed in groups on produce in its peak ripeness. Anything that is full of life is the target for these pests that have a four-to-five-week lifespan but do oh-so-much damage. Then they lay eggs so their larvae can hatch next year and start the process all over again!

Predators to soil health are akin to the predators of our souls. Thomas Aquinas, who was an Italian philosopher and theologian, referred to these dangers as "the world, the flesh, and the devil." In the Council of Trent, Aquinas called them "the implacable enemies of the soul."[25]

Here is a brief explanation of each of these enemies of the soul:

24. "8 Facts."
25. "World, the Flesh."

- The world—ideas, systems, stories, and values contrary to God's design.

- The flesh—disordered desires (gluttony, sexual immorality, etc.).

- The devil—the personal enemy of God and humans, the father of lies, a fallen angel, who comes to "steal and kill and destroy" (John 10:10).[26]

Our first summer with our new garden beds was the summer that we dealt with the biggest amount of pests (*before* we came back from vacation and discovered the nut grass!). In one summer, we dealt with stunted plants (OK, that was our fault), gophers, squirrels, ants, aphids, and high temperatures. We harvested very few crops that summer because of all of the pests and temperature issues.

Here's a story for you. I planted four Thousandhead Kale seeds in the designated area in our garden beds. I was so excited to plant this new kale because the leaves were supposed to grow much bigger than my head. I planted them two feet apart, watered them, and waited. Within a week or so, the seedlings sprouted! We were off to a great start, me and these new kale plants. Then, one morning, I noticed one seedling had completely vanished during the night—there was not a trace of it. I concluded it must have been a squirrel that had eaten the seedling down to the ground. The next day, another one disappeared, much like the first. Sure enough, a couple of days later, I came by, and only one Thousandhead Kale seedling was left! Where the third one had once been, there was a small mound of dirt in the middle of a circle in the dirt. Aha! A ground squirrel was to blame for all of this! He was underground, sucking the plants through a hole he was making in the ground and dragging the seedlings into the ground to eat them in secret.

I got desperate. I had heard of people praying over their houseplants and garden plants. And I had judged them in my heart. (OK, not badly, though). Well, I did it. I laid one of my hands on the one remaining Thousandhead Kale seedling, and I interceded for the life of this last kale plant. I prayed over it and

26. NIV.

blessed it. I asked for protection. I asked for it to live and produce a fruitful crop.

And do you know over one year later this plant is still going strong and has been one of the most bountiful crops in our garden this year? It has blessed many people with its produce (even my kale-mocking neighbor who once at our neighborhood block party playfully gave me a cookie wrapped up in a large kale leaf and told me he brought me a "kale cookie"). The power of blessing and prayer, y'all!

The blessed Thousandhead Kale plant.

All of these factors reduce the ability for the soil to support plant life and crop productivity. We must be on alert and watching, for ways the world, the flesh, and the devil are seeking to draw us away from God and unleash disease and destruction on our hearts.

6

Our Hearts, a Gift to Be Stewarded Well

GOD HAS GIVEN EACH of us such an immensely generous gift. He's given each of us a heart to have the free will to cultivate. His design was for our hearts to be a beautiful, lush garden teeming with life because we are drawing upon Him for all things. But we have all fallen short and have chosen sin, which brings death into our hearts and our gardens, and it's a battle to the end. Interestingly, much like the serpent was bent on wreaking havoc on the life that God created by entering the garden to steal, kill, and destroy, so God is deeply desiring that we abide with Him and stay connected to Him in every moment. It's how He made us. He knows best. It's John 15:

> I am the Real Vine and my Father is the Farmer. He cuts off every branch of me that doesn't bear grapes. And every branch that is grape-bearing he prunes back so it will bear even more. You are already pruned back by the message I have spoken. Live in me. Make your home in me just as I do in you. In the same way that a branch can't bear grapes by itself but only by being joined with the vine, you can't bear fruit unless you are joined with me. I am the Vine, you are the branches. When you're joined

with me and I with you, the relationship is intimate and organic, the harvest is sure to be abundant. Separated, you can't produce a thing. Anyone who separates from me is deadwood, gathered up and thrown on the bonfire. But if you make yourselves at home with me and my words are at home in you, you can be sure that whatever you ask will be listened to and acted upon. This is how my Father shows who he is—when you produce grapes, when you mature as my disciples. I've loved you the way my Father has loved me. Make yourselves at home in my life. If you keep my commands, you'll remain intimately at home in my love. That's what I've done—kept my Father's commands and made myself at home in his love. I've told you these things for a purpose: that my joy might be your joy, and your joy wholly mature. This is my command: Love one another the way I have loved you. This is the very best way to love. Put your life on the line for your friends. You are my friends when you do the things I command you. I'm no longer calling you servants because servants don't understand what their master is thinking and planning. No, I've made you friends because I've let you in on everything I've heard from the Father. You didn't choose me, remember; I chose you, and put you in the world to bear fruit, fruit that won't spoil. As fruit bearers, whatever you ask the Father in relation to me, he gives you. But remember the root command: Love one another (John 15: 1–17).[1]

God desires for us to stay intimately connected to Him and tend to our hearts for His glory.

God is the One with the original plan, the original Master Planner of gardens. He even began human life in the middle of a garden! I don't think that's just coincidence.

We must be vigilant guards of our hearts as Proverbs tells us, as a good gardener watches over his garden. Pests come to steal, kill, and destroy. They do this by eating the crops, feeding on the roots or poisoning the soil so it adversely affects the plant. It takes

1. MSG.

both time and attention to watch over our souls and gardens. We *must* put in the time. The temptation is to put it off until later.

Later this afternoon when I have a free moment.

Later this week I'll spend time with God when I have some margin.

Next month before the weeds get *really* bad.

Ah, never mind. I'll plant a garden next spring.

Do you see how easy it is to become too relaxed about watching over our hearts and gardens? We must be proactive, not reactive. We must have some rhythms put in place that anchor us in taking time to tend to our hearts and gardens. It's time and consistency over a length of time. We can't afford not to be disciplined in this area. Gardens, yes, those are an option in our day and age. But watching over the garden of our hearts? Not an option.

It's *vital*.

For us, that looks like a weekly sabbath, where we intentionally cease from striving and working and rest and delight in God. Also, throughout the week, I've adopted different rhythms to pause and reflect on what's going on in my heart. I love to journal, and I've found it to be an important practice. Putting my thoughts, prayers, and emotions to paper is a therapeutic exercise. The Prayer of Examen has been a helpful tool in the evenings. I once heard a quote about a theologian who said that he spent 50 percent of his time living his life and 50 percent reflecting on his life. That may seem excessive (and frankly impossible, at least for this mama of five!), but I think the point was that we need to slow down enough to take inventory of our lives, how we're living them, what's going on in our souls, bring issues to light with God and others, and work through them. If we don't, our soil will become damaged, sour and uninhabitable for life to thrive.

The past year, my eye has been drawn to trellises. I felt the Lord highlighting them to me when I was asking Him how I was to order my life. "You must trellis your life," I heard Him say to me. The purpose of a trellis is to support plants that are climbing, but can't stand on their own. The trellis is the support it needs to climb high and be stable. In today's world, we need this. We need anchoring rhythms where we are checking in with God and with our hearts. One popular resource that has been helpful to many is developing a rule of life. A rule of life is a simple construct that you can create that helps you develop and keep rhythms in your life which support what you're cultivating—sabbath, community, stewardship, etc. A great book to give you an overview is *The Common Rule: Habits of Purpose for an Age of Distraction* by Justin Whitmel Early. Also, Garden Church in Huntington Beach, California, has a great resource to put it into practice.[2]

One specific and practical way of watching over your soul is to obey this command in Eph 4:26–27:

> Be angry [at sin—at immorality, at injustice, at ungodly behavior], YET DO NOT SIN; do not let your anger [cause you shame, nor allow it to] last until the sun goes down. And do not give the devil an opportunity [to lead you into sin by holding a grudge, or nurturing anger, or harboring resentment, or cultivating bitterness].[3]

There's something about searching our souls before God before we go to bed at night—if there is anything you've let fester throughout the day with your spouse, a child, a coworker, etc., *deal with it*. Don't let the sun go down on your anger. If you do, it's like you're saying, "OK, devil, here's a hand in climbing up into the places of my heart." Yikes! Scripture plainly says that we can give the devil a foothold. As in rock climbing, a foothold is "a strong or favorable position from which further advances or progress may be made."[4] OK, *that* should make us think twice about letting the sun go down on our anger. That terrifies me to think of lending a hand for the devil to put his foot into my life and make progress or further advancement in my heart. Lord, have mercy!

2. "Rule of Life Course."

3. AMP.

4. "Foothold."

IN CONCLUSION: SOIL 101

This morning, while the house was still quiet, I felt beckoned outside to pull weeds in the summer garden. The early summer mornings when the sun is young in the sky and it's not yet scorching the ground is the best time of the day, in my opinion. The birds chirp their greeting at me, and it's so, so quiet.

Morning time in the flower garden.

My mind falls to meditating on these tidbits I've been learning. Let's be good soil with sound souls, where we hear the Word, understand it (and grasp and receive and keep it) with an honest and good heart. Remember to pray before opening up the Word for your heart to be good soil—maybe you need to confess and "pull some weeds" before digging into the Word and asking God to speak to you and be free. Remember that just hearing the Word is not enough—we must move on to understanding. For the glory of God and the furthering of His Kingdom, may we be good soil that produces an abundant crop. It's worth every effort, my friends!

Bibliography

"8 Facts You Should Know About Japanese Beetle Control, Traps, Grubs, and Their Life Cycle." *Oasis Turf and Tree.* https://www.oasisturf.com/blog/8-facts-you-should-know-about-japanese-beetle-control-traps-grubs-and-their-life-cycle.

"Augustine of Hippo Quotes." https://www.goodreads.com/quotes.

Bonhoeffer, Dietrich. *Letters and Papers from Prison.* New York: Touchstone, 1997.

Clarke, Regina. "'No One Can Make You Feel Inferior without Your Consent.'—Eleanor Roosevelt." *Medium*, July 21, 2018. https://medium.com/illumination-curated/no-one-can-make-you-feel-inferior-without-your-consent-eleanor-roosevelt-842e552e52c6#:~:text=%E2%80%9CNo%20one%20can%20make%20you,Regina%20Clarke%20%7C%20Curated%20Newsletters%20%7C%20Medium.

Comer, John Mark. *Live No Lies.* Colorado Springs: Waterbrook, 2021.

Comer, John Mark. *The Ruthless Elimination of Hurry.* Colorado Springs: Waterbrook, 2019.

"Cornell CALS." *College of Agriculture and Life Sciences.* Cornell University. https://cals.cornell.edu.

Cost, Ben. "Americans Have Fewer Friends than Ever Before: Study." *New York Post*, July 27, 2021. https://nypost.com/2021/07/27/americans-have-fewer-friends-than-ever-before-study/.

Critical Skills. "Critical Skills and Strongholds: Gear Up. Get Practice. Be Equipped." https://savehealdeliver.us/.

Dirt to Dinner. www.dirt-to-dinner.com.

Dixon, Francis. "Study 1 The Farmer, the Seed, and the Soils." *Words of Life.* https://www.wordsoflife.co.uk/bible-studies/study-1-the-farmer-the-seed-and-the-soils/.

Elliot, Elisabeth. *A Path Through Suffering.* Grand Rapids: Revell, 2003.

Ersek, Kaitlyn. "The 6 Essential Nutrients for Healthy Plants." *Holganix*, September 11, 2012. https://www.holganix.com/blog/the-6-essential-nutrients-for-healthy-plants#:~:text=These%20six%20essential%20nutrients%20are,then%20organize%20into%20plant%20tissue.

"Fallow-ground." *Bible Study Tools.* https://www.biblestudytools.com/dictionary/fallow-ground/.

"Foothold." Collins Online Dictionary, 2024. https://www.collinsdictionary.com/dictionary/english/foothold.

Fuller, Kristen. "How Clutter and Mental Health are Connected." *Very Well Mind*, August 21, 2023. https://www.verywellmind.com/decluttering-our-house-to-cleanse-our-minds-5101511.

Gaultiere, Bill. "Dallas Willard's Definitions and Quotes." https://www.soulshepherding.org/dallas-willards-definitions/.

Hamer, Ashley. "What Would Happen if the Sun Disappeared?" *Discovery*, August 1, 2019. https://www.discovery.com/science/What-Would-Happen-If-the-Sun-Disappeared.

Hirt, Heribert. "Healthy Soil for Healthy Plants for Healthy Humans." *Embo Press*, July 31, 2020. https://www.embopress.org/doi/full/10.15252/embr.202051069.

Jacoby, Richard, et al. "The Role of Soil Microorganisms in Plant Mineral Nutrition—Current Knowledge and Future Directions." https://www.frontiersin.org/journals/plant-science/articles/10.3389/fpls.2017.01617/full.

Jeffries, Stuart. "Why Too Much Choice Is Stressing Us Out." *The Guardian.* October 21, 2015. https://www.theguardian.com/lifeandstyle/2015/oct/21/choice-stressing-us-out-dating-partners-monopolies.

Johnson, Jan. *Abundant Simplicity.* Grand Rapids: InterVarsity, 2011.

"Light Deprivation: What Happens if You Don't Get Enough Sunlight?" *Carex*, September 22, 2023. https://carex.com/blogs/resources/light-deprivation-what-happens-if-you-don-t-get-enough-sunlight?srsltid=AfmBOooruHTG2-TTiHdNGTUhNoCXoqvWSFgN_zDiUqS1_Vn5coswDlo4.

"Margin." Merriam-Webster Online Dictionary, 2024. https://www.merriam-webster.com/dictionary/margin.

"Matthew 13:23 Translation and Meaning." https://www.quotescosmos.com/bible/bible-verses/Matthew-13-23.html.

"Missing the Mark." *Living Truth*, May 25, 2018. https://livingtruth.ca/blogs/devotionals/missing-the-mark.

Olive, Dalton. "Arranging Our Days: No Wasted Time". *Medium*, November 18, 2018. https://daltonolive93.medium.com/arranging-our-days-no-wasted-time-b9d5b767161a.

"Panim/Paneh: Seek My Face." www.hebrewwordlessons.scom.

Papa, Rocco. "Jim Carrey Revealed His Religious Beliefs During an Emotional Speech to a Room of Inmates." *The Things.* May 29, 2023. https://www.thethings.com/jim-carrey-revealed-his-religious-beliefs-during-an-emotional-speech-to-a-room-of-inmates/#:~:text=In%20an%20interview%20with%20CBS%20News%2C%20Carrey%20said,place%2C%20or%20you%20are%20in%20an%20unloving%20place.

The Pastorate. "Incubator Sessions: Darren Rouanzoin—Disrupting Comforts, Identifying Compromise and Consecration." *YouTube*, June 21, 2022. https://www.youtube.com/watch?app=desktop&v=u9_DQQ5f51s&ab_channel=ThePastorate.

Peterson, Jordan. *12 Rules for Life: An Antidote to Chaos*. Toronto: Random House Canada, 2018.

Pilat, Dan, and Sekoul Krastev. "Why Do We Have a Harder Time Choosing When We Have More Options?" *The Decision Lab*. https://thedecisionlab.com/biases/choice-overload-bias.

Ramirez, Mary Ann. "Nut Grass: Three Experts' Solutions to One of the Worst Weeds." *Los Angeles Times*. March 7, 2013. https://www.latimes.com/home/la-lh-nutgrass-nutsedge-weed-control-20130304-story.html.

"Reading Before the Face of God." *King's Chapel*. https://kingschapel.net/reading-before-the-face-of-god/.

JP. "Repentance Activation." *YouTube*, August 2, 2012. https://www.youtube.com/watch?v=ma6tX21Pycw.

RJM. "Matthew 13:1–9; 18–23." *Lectionary Greek* (blog), July 10, 2023. http://lectionarygreek.blogspot.com/2011/07/matthew-1318-23.html?m=1.

"Rule of Life Course." Garden Church. https://gardenchurch.thinkific.com/courses/discipleship-formation.

Scazzero, Peter. "Peter Scazzero Quotes." *Quote Fancy*. https://quotefancy.com/quote/2440324/Peter-Scazzero-Rabbi-Zusya-when-he-was-an-old-man-said-In-the-coming-world-they-will-not.

South Beach Church Slogan. https://www.southbeachchurch.org.

Southern, Matt. G. "Pinterest Reaches 60% of US Women; Here's What They're Searching For." *Search Engine Journal*, February 29, 2020. https://www.searchenginejournal.com/pinterest-reaches-60-of-us-women-heres-what-theyre-searching-for/352446/.

Sullivan, Andrew. "I Used to Be a Human Being." *New York Magazine*, September 19, 2016. https://nymag.com/intelligencer/2016/09/andrew-sullivan-my-distraction-sickness-and-yours.html.

Steiner, Ann. "Comparison is the Thief of Joy." *Active Christianity*. https://activechristianity.org/comparison-is-the-thief-of-joy.

Swenson, Richard A. *Margin: Restoring Emotional, Physical, Financial and Time Reserves to Overloaded Lives*. Colorado Springs: NavPress, 2004.

"The World, the Flesh, and the Devil." *Wikipedia*. Revised May 17, 2024. https://en.wikipedia.org/wiki/The_world,_the_flesh,_and_the_devil.

University of California Agriculture and Natural Resources. "Fertilizers vs. Soil Amendments." https://ipm.ucanr.edu/TOOLS/TURF/SITEPREP/amenfert.html#:~:text=Fertilizers%20improve%20the%20supply%20of,and%20soil%20amendments%20is%20confusing.

Willard, Dallas. "Dallas Willard Quotes about Heart." *AZ Quotes*. https://www.azquotes.com/author/15666-Dallas_Willard/tag/heart.

"Water Salinization." *ScienceDirect*. https://www.sciencedirect.com/topics/agricultural-and-biological-sciences/water-salinization.

Weber, J. D. Tingey, and C. Andersen. "Plant Response to Air Pollution." *Science Inventory*. United States Environmental Protection Agency, March 9, 2021. https://cfpub.epa.gov/si/si_public_record_Report.cfm?Lab=NHEE RL&dirEntryId=50437.

Wickey, Brenda. "Writers' Corner: See the Beauty in It." *Sturgis Journal*, May 25, 2019. https://www.sturgisjournal.com/story/entertainment/local/2019 /05/25/writers-corner-see-beauty-in/5062365007/.

Willard, Dallas. *Renovation of the Heart*. Colorado Springs: NavPress, 2012.

Wilson, Tim. "Les Miserables (1998) Jean Valjean: Bought with a Price. Opening Scene, Powerful." YouTube, March 10, 2021. Video. https://www. youtube.com/watch?v=BQKQ5xTbYZU.

Words of Life Ministries. "Words of Life Ministries." https://wordsoflife.co.uk.